By God's Design: Walking in Purpose, Not Permission

Written by Dr. LaQuita Parks
International Best-Selling Author & Publisher

"Write the vision and make it plain on tablets, that he may run who reads it."
—Habakkuk 2:2 (NKJV)

Copyright © 2025 by Dr. LaQuita Parks
All rights reserved.

No part of this publication may be reproduced, stored in a retrieval system, or transmitted in any form or by any means—electronic, mechanical, photocopy, recording, or otherwise—without prior written permission from the author or publisher, except for brief quotations used in reviews or articles.

ISBN: 978-1-959667-84-1
LCCN: 2025917653

Published by:
Pa-Pro-Vi Publishing
www.paprovipublishing.com

Cover Design by: Dr. LaQuita Parks
Edited by: Pa-Pro-Vi Publishing Editorial Team

Disclaimer: This memoir is based on actual events in the author's life. The author has changed certain names, locations, and identifying details to protect privacy. Any resemblance to actual persons, living or dead, or actual events is coincidental unless explicitly stated. The author and publisher assume no responsibility for any outcomes or actions taken by readers based on the content of this work.

Printed in the United States of America

"God doesn't call the qualified; He qualifies the called."

Table of Contents

Foreword
Acknowledgements
In Loving Memory
Introduction
Chapter 1 – When the Story Didn't End
Chapter 2 – The Mayo Clinic Chronicles
Chapter 3 – Faith in the Waiting Room
Chapter 4 – Grief Times Two + One
Chapter 5 – The Strength of a Limp
Chapter 6 – When God Changes the Prescription
Chapter 7 – The Birth of Pa-Pro-Vi Publishing
Chapter 8 – The Ministry of Storytelling
Chapter 9 – From Thought to Realization
Chapter 10 – The Power of Collective Healing
Chapter 11 – Trusting the Voice Within
Chapter 12 – Permission Denied Purpose Approved
Chapter 13 – When Your Walk Makes Others Uncomfortable
Chapter 14 – The Weight of Being Chosen
Chapter 15 – Obedience Over Outcome
Chapter 16 – Raising Voices Not Just Books
Chapter 17 – The Unseen Victories
Chapter 18 – Resting Without Guilt
Chapter 19 – My Walk, My Worship
Chapter 20 – By Gods Design

Afterword
Scripture References
About the Author

Foreword

I am honored to have the privilege of writing the forward for this book. It's personal for me because it's for the only friend I have ever had. I am not qualified to give this forward the scholarly literary honor that the author and the book so richly deserves. Nevertheless I will make a few times effort to honor the author and the literature.

Purpose is not something granted—it is something discovered, embraced, and boldly walked out. In a world that too often demands validation before vision, and approval before action, Dr. LaQuita Parks offers a powerful and necessary reminder: you do not need permission to be who you were created to be.

In 'Walking in Purpose, Not by Permission,' Dr. Parks invites us into her journey—one marked not by ease or privilege, but by resilience, pain, and resolved determination. With rare and raw honesty and a voice both compassionate and courageous, she confronts the false narratives that have silenced too many for too long. This book is not just a personal testimony; it is a call to action. A call to live intentionally, to rise from trauma, trials, troubles, and tribulations to claim the purpose that is rightfully yours.

Dr. Parks doesn't ask for your sympathy. She asks you to look inward. She challenges you to see beyond your limitations, your fears, and the permissions you've been waiting on. Her words speak directly to the dreamer, the doer, the wounded, and the weary—and she reminds us that purpose is not passive. It is chosen. It is lived. Dr Parks is a perfect warrior of perfecting her walk without limitations to achieve her purpose.

Whether you are just beginning your journey or standing at a crossroads, this book will awaken something in you. It will stir your soul, shift your mindset, and most importantly, empower you to walk in purpose—with or without permission.

This book will enlighten, encourage, and engross your soul, because it's motivated by the spiritual permission to walk with God's purpose in His mission. Dr Parks' walk is not limited because the steps of a good woman are directed by the Lord (PS.37:23).

Robert E. Brooks

Acknowledgements

To my children—thank you for being my greatest reason to keep going. You have given me purpose, laughter, and the kind of love that heals in places words can't reach. You are my living reminders that God's promises are true, and every sacrifice has been worth it.

To my beautiful grandchildren—you are the joy that lights up my days. Your little smiles, hugs, and "I love you's" are treasures that remind me how much more there is to live for. I pray that my life shows you what it means to walk boldly in God's design.

To my dear friends and unwavering supporters, thank you for praying for me, cheering for me, and holding me up when I felt like I couldn't stand. Your love has been an anchor in the storm and a celebration in the sunshine.

To every author who has trusted me with your story—know that it has been an honor beyond words. You have allowed me into sacred spaces of your life, and together, we have turned pain into purpose and pages into power. Your courage inspires me daily, and I am humbled that you chose me to help bring your vision to life.

To all of you—family, friends, supporters, and storytellers—this book is as much yours as it is mine. Without you, the journey would have been lonelier, the victories smaller, and the mission incomplete. From the depths of my heart, thank you for believing in me, walking with me, and trusting the God who designed us for more.

In Loving Memory

My Grandmother – My Rock of Faith

"She is clothed with strength and dignity; she can laugh at the days to come." – Proverbs 31:25

Grandma, your faith was a steady anchor in my life. You taught me that love is shown in the little things—the extra slice of cake, the long talks at the kitchen table, the prayers whispered when no one else was listening. Your strength carried generations, and your quiet wisdom shaped the woman I am today. Every time I choose faith over fear, I hear your voice guiding me.

My Mother – My First Teacher of Love

"Her children rise up and call her blessed." – Proverbs 31:28

Mama, you taught me resilience before I even understood the word. You stood by me in hospital rooms, celebrated my victories, and believed in me when the world didn't. Losing you left an ache that words cannot fill, but your love still surrounds me like a warm embrace. Every time I stand tall in my calling, I honor the woman who first told me I could.

Caryn – My Sister in Spirit

"A friend loves at all times, and a brother is born for a time of adversity." – Proverbs 17:17

Caryn, you were more than my friend—you were my sister in spirit. You knew my heart, my dreams, and my struggles, and you stood by me in them all. Your laughter was medicine, your advice was gold, and your presence was a gift. Though you are no longer here to walk beside me, I carry your voice in my heart, urging me to keep going, to keep loving, and to keep being me.

You Are Forever Part of My Story

Grandma, Mama, and Caryn—this book is for you. Every chapter carries pieces of your love, your lessons, and your legacy. You are not just part of my past—you are woven into my present and my future.

Introduction

Nine years ago, I shared my truth in *Walking Limitations by Other People's Definition*—a raw, transparent telling of how one medical mistake stole my mobility but never my will to keep walking. That story marked a beginning. It was my declaration that no longer would I live bound by the labels others gave me. But what I didn't know then was just how much further God intended to take me—not by permission of man, but by His divine design.

Since then, life has brought its share of unexpected valleys and sacred mountaintop moments. I spent months in and out of the Mayo Clinic in Jacksonville, Florida—my body still wrestling with chronic pain that often felt louder than my faith. But in those sterile hospital rooms, between the needles and the diagnoses, I found something more powerful than pain: *I found purpose*. I learned that healing doesn't always mean a cure; sometimes, it means learning how to live *with* the pain, and still move forward anyway.

In 2009, I lost both my grandmother and my mother—seventeen days apart. But it wasn't until the years following *Walking Limitations* that I truly had to learn how to live without them. Grief is a strange teacher. It doesn't just sit with you in your sadness—it reshapes who you are. Their absence left a void, but their love left a legacy. It is through their strength, their nurturing, their wisdom, that I continue to rise. I carry them with me in every step I take, and in every life I help transform.

In the midst of that continued journey—*Pa-Pro-Vi Publishing* was born. It started with one simple belief: that pain, when processed through faith and courage, can become progress... and eventually, victory. Through this ministry of storytelling, I have been able to help hundreds of authors—many of whom never imagined their voices could carry this far—bring their stories from *a thought to a realization.* From children's books to trauma memoirs, from poetry to powerful anthologies, we have published stories that are now changing lives around the world.

And through every page, every testimony, every coaching session, I am reminded: this walk was never meant to follow someone else's blueprint. I am walking—yes, with a limp, yes, with chronic pain—but I am walking *on purpose, by God's design.* No longer seeking permission to be who He called me to be.

Today, I live with the understanding that I am not broken—I am built differently. I am not walking a path of perfection—I am walking a path of *promise.* And as I continue to guide others to uncover the power of their own stories, I know one thing for sure: *My walk is not defined by what happened to me. It is defined by the One who walks with me.*

Chapter 1
When the Story Didn't End

"Being confident of this very thing, that He who has begun a good work in you will complete it until the day of Jesus Christ."
—Philippians 1:6 (NKJV)

In 2016, I did something brave. Something bold. Something I didn't realize would become one of the greatest turning points in my healing journey.

Seven years after the unimaginable loss of my grandmother and my mother—seventeen days apart—I gave birth to something new. Something that didn't cry or crawl but bled from the deepest parts of me: *Walking Limitations by Other People's Definition.* That book was more than a manuscript—it was a confession. A declaration. A release.

For the first time in my life, I stood fully exposed, revealing the hidden layers of my story—the parts that I had spent decades trying to forget. I wrote about the medical trauma that changed my life when I was just a little girl. I was four years old, going into the hospital to have my tonsils removed. What should have been a simple procedure turned into a lifelong sentence of pain and physical limitation. A nurse jabbed me in the thigh with a needle—seemingly without care, without thought—and I never walked the same again. I had to learn how to walk all over again, but no one taught me how to emotionally recover from what was lost.

I told that story in *Walking Limitations*—the childhood trauma that altered my body and shaped my worldview. But that wasn't the only story I told. I also revealed the personal limitations I placed on myself—the fears, the insecurities, the toxic relationships. I shared the emotional and sometimes physical abuse I experienced in my marriage. I wrote about the years I spent trying to hide behind strength while silently suffocating from pain. The girl with the different leg. The woman with the different walk. The mother with the broken heart trying to raise whole children.

It was one of me and three of them—my three beautiful children. And life was tough.

I was doing my best to raise them right. To give them a life better than the one I had. But somewhere along the way, I started to notice something uncomfortable, something I didn't want to admit at first: I was unknowingly passing my limitations onto them.

I saw it in how I spoke to them when I was tired and overwhelmed. I saw it in the expectations I placed on their shoulders—expectations born not out of love, but out of fear. Fear that they would hurt like I had. Fear that the world would treat them the way it had treated me. I wanted to protect them, but my protection came with pressure. I realized that I wasn't just parenting my children—I was parenting my pain.

The truth hit me hard: I couldn't break inherited traits while still being bound by them.

And so, *Walking Limitations* became the start—not the end—of something bigger than I had ever imagined. It gave me the courage to be honest, not just on the page, but in real life. It helped me begin the process of healing, but healing, I quickly learned, is not linear. It's layered. It's painful. And it's often inconvenient.

When the book was released, people reached out to tell me how it impacted them. How it gave them the language to tell their own stories. How it helped them confront their own pain. But while everyone was celebrating the book, I was sitting in silence with the parts of my story that still felt unfinished. Parts that weren't in the book because I hadn't yet faced them myself.

Although I had a stable job and a good reputation, something was missing. There was an ache inside of me—a deep yearning for something more. I had obeyed the gospel years before, but I knew that it was time for me to get serious about my walk with God. Not just attending church. Not just quoting scriptures. But surrendering—completely and wholeheartedly.

You see, obedience is one thing. Devotion is another.

And I knew that if I was going to step into the next season of my life—if I was truly going to walk without apology—I had to stop living halfway. I had to let God deal with the parts of me I didn't want to deal with. The bitterness I was still holding. The unforgiveness I had buried so deeply I thought it was gone. The brokenness I had normalized.

So, I went back to the beginning. Not the beginning of the pain—but the beginning of my purpose.

God didn't make a mistake when He allowed me to survive that needle. He didn't forget me when I lost my mother and grandmother. He didn't abandon me in my marriage. No—He was molding me. Refining me. Teaching me how to walk in purpose, not permission.

And that purpose began to unfold in ways I couldn't have predicted. What started as one book soon became a ministry. A movement. Pa-Pro-Vi Publishing was born from my pain—founded on the belief that stories heal and truth transforms. I began helping other people do what I had done—tell their stories, confront their limitations, and discover the purpose in their pain. And in doing so, I began to heal more deeply than I ever could have on my own.

But let me be clear: I'm still healing. I'm still learning. I still have bad days when the pain in my body reminds me of that hospital room, and I still have moments when the emotional scars of my past try to tell me I'm not enough. But I've learned to walk anyway.

I walk with faith.
I walk with fire.
I walk with freedom.

And though my walk may be different, it is divinely designed.

This chapter of my life—the one that began after *Walking Limitations*—has taught me that our stories don't end when the book closes. Sometimes, that's when the real work begins. The work of living out what you've confessed. The work of applying the truth you've written down. The work of allowing God to use your pain to heal someone else's.

I no longer view my walking limitations as a curse. I see them as a calling.

God didn't heal me in the way I expected—but He healed me in the way I needed. He gave me strength to endure. Vision to build. And boldness to speak.

Almost ten years later, I am still overcoming my walking limitation—but now I am using it to help others overcome theirs. That is the power of testimony. That is the gift of obedience. That is what happens when the story doesn't end, but instead continues in purpose.

Chapter 2
The Mayo Clinic Chronicles

"And He said to me, 'My grace is sufficient for you, for My strength is made perfect in weakness.' Therefore most gladly I will rather boast in my infirmities, that the power of Christ may rest upon me.
—2 Corinthians 12:9 (NKJV)

"While you are not dying, you are suffering."

2019 was the year I turned fifty, and I decided I wasn't going to wait for someone else to celebrate me. I had spent too much of my life waiting—waiting to be seen, waiting to be chosen, waiting to be validated, waiting to feel worthy. But fifty brought a new mindset. I had lived through enough to know that life doesn't promise applause, and I had learned to clap for myself.

So, I threw myself a party.

Not just any party—a party to remember. I invited fifty people to celebrate fifty years of survival, struggle, strength, and God's sustaining grace. I told everyone to dress up. Not just Sunday-best, but elegant. It was a night of laughter, sparkle, and joy. I looked good. I felt good. I danced like the weight of life hadn't been pressing on me for decades. I smiled like I wasn't carrying silent pain. That night, I was more than my diagnosis, more than my limitations. I was a woman embracing her now.

But what I didn't know then was that only six weeks later, I would be fighting another invisible battle. One that would bring me to the edge of medical uncertainty and emotional exhaustion. One that would take me to the Mayo Clinic in Jacksonville, Florida, again and again from November 2019 to February 2020.

I had only just returned to work in July after being out on medical leave—again. It had become a cycle I knew too well: work, pain, time off, recovery, return, repeat. But still, I had hope. Still, I kept going. That's what you do when you're used to pain—you learn how to keep pushing through it. But that October, just weeks after celebrating my 50th birthday, something changed. I started getting sick again—sicker than usual.

It began slowly, with symptoms that didn't make sense. Pain. Fatigue. Swelling. Discomfort. Then came the doctor's visits. Then the ER—three times in one week. I was passed from specialist to specialist, all of them trying to connect dots that didn't seem to form any picture. My body was speaking a language no one could translate.

Eventually, my primary care doctor looked me in the eyes and said, "You need the Mayo Clinic."

I had heard of Mayo. I knew it was for "serious" cases—complicated ones. People went there when answers were hard to find. So off I went, unsure, scared, and completely unprepared for the journey ahead.

Each trip to Jacksonville lasted a week. And each day of those weeks was filled with appointments—sometimes five, sometimes six in a single day. Early mornings. Long waits. Endless blood draws. CT scans. MRIs. Tests I didn't even know existed. Nurses trying to find veins that rolled away like they were dodging needles. My arms became a patchwork of bruises and tape. I felt like a medical science project—poked, prodded, scanned, evaluated.

And I was tired. Bone-tired. Soul-tired.

The kind of tired you can't sleep off.

It wasn't just physical—it was emotional. It was the weight of uncertainty. The fear of not knowing. The isolation of sitting in a hospital room with sterile walls and silent prayers. I was not just dealing with doctors—I was dealing with the possibility that this time, I might not bounce back.

I didn't feel strong. I didn't feel like a warrior. I felt like a woman unraveling, stitch by fragile stitch.

And you know what wasn't on my mind during that time?

Walking Limitations.

The book that had changed my life—the story that had cracked me wide open—I had completely forgotten about it. Not because it wasn't important, but because I didn't have the capacity to think about anything outside of surviving the moment.

Then one day, my phone rang. It was a voice I hadn't heard in years—a woman I knew from high school.

After the usual "how are you" check-in, she paused.

"I have a question," she said.

"Sure," I answered, a little hesitant.

"How did you publish your book?"

I was quiet for a second, caught off guard.

"You mean *Walking Limitations*?"

"Yes," she said. "I've had this idea for a book for a while, but I didn't know what direction to go in… until I remembered you had written one. I need your help."

I looked around the room I was sitting in—medical papers in my lap, bandages on my arms, uncertainty thick in the air. Part of me wanted to say, "I can't right now. I'm at the Mayo Clinic. I don't have the bandwidth."

But something in me said yes.

And when I said yes to helping her, something shifted.

I got out of my head and into my purpose. Helping her gave me a momentary escape from my own pain. It reminded me of who I was outside of my diagnosis. It reminded me that even when I feel empty, I still have something to give.

That conversation became a spark. That spark became a project. That project became a business. And that business became a ministry.

Pa-Pro-Vi Publishing was born—not in a boardroom, not during a strategy session, not after months of planning. It was born in the middle of my suffering. In a Mayo Clinic waiting room. While I was bleeding and bruised and trying to hold myself together, God was birthing something inside of me that would help others heal.

That's how He works sometimes.

Right in the middle of your waiting room, He introduces your purpose.

Between doctor's visits and silent cries, He whispers destiny.

On my final trip to Mayo, after months of tests, the doctor looked at me with compassion in his eyes and said, "While you are not dying, you are suffering."

He didn't sugarcoat it.

He didn't dismiss it.

And for once, I felt seen.

I wasn't imagining it. I wasn't being dramatic. I wasn't exaggerating.

I was suffering.

But that suffering wasn't in vain. It was doing something.

It was building something.

It was refining something.

Pain has a way of pulling you into the presence of God in ways comfort never can. At the Mayo Clinic, I learned to trust God not for quick answers but for sustaining grace. I learned that sometimes the miracle isn't in the cure—it's in the courage to keep hoping. To keep believing. To keep showing up for life even when life feels like it's slipping away.

The Mayo Clinic became more than a hospital to me—it became a holy place. A place where God met me in my uncertainty. A place where He reminded me that while my body may be limited, my purpose is not.

From that moment on, I knew I had to do more than survive—I had to serve.

And not just any kind of service.

I had to help people tell their stories.

Because when you share your story, you not only heal yourself—you give someone else permission to heal too.

That's what Pa-Pro-Vi is about: Pain. Progress. Victory.

The pain I experienced at Mayo became progress when I said yes to that phone call. That progress turned into victory when I watched that woman hold her finished book in her hands and cry tears of release.

It started with one.

And it hasn't stopped since.

Chapter 3
Faith in the Waiting Room

"Wait on the LORD; Be of good courage, And He shall strengthen your heart; Wait, I say, on the LORD!"
—Psalm 27:14 (NKJV)

They say patience is a virtue. I've heard that for as long as I can remember. But what they don't tell you is how hard patience is when your body is tired, your heart is broken, and your soul is weary from the weight of unanswered questions. Growing up, I had no real concept of patience—I was more familiar with the ache of *waiting*. And not just waiting, but *impatiently* waiting.

Waiting has been the undercurrent of my life.

Waiting to walk again.
Waiting to be seen.
Waiting for healing.
Waiting to be loved.
Waiting to be chosen.
Waiting for my name to be called.

I've waited in medical offices, legal offices, emergency rooms, and relationship corners where love never showed up. I've waited for answers that didn't come, and I've waited in silence that felt louder than any diagnosis.

But through it all, I've also learned this: waiting doesn't always mean being still. Sometimes, waiting is active. Sometimes, it's holy.

And most importantly, waiting has taught me something deeper than patience—it has taught me *faith*.

I've always liked a bit of background noise when I work—music, TV, soft sounds to fill the silence. One afternoon, while working on a manuscript, a hospital commercial played in the background. A man was giving a heartfelt testimonial, praising the staff who had saved his life. I wasn't really paying attention until I heard the hospital's name: Grady Memorial Hospital.

I froze.

Then came the second commercial. This time it was a woman, her voice trembling with gratitude as she shared how the hospital had rescued her from the brink. She called it a miracle.

I stopped dead in my tracks.

Because my story with Grady was not one of miracles. It was one of trauma.

It was *the place*—the beginning of my life in the waiting room. I had entered Grady Hospital just weeks after my fourth birthday, a little girl with two healthy legs and a bright future. But when I left, I was permanently changed. A botched medical procedure—an improperly administered injection—left me with a life-altering injury. I was crippled. And no one could undo it.

The commercials didn't feel like advertisements. They felt like gaslighting.

My hands trembled. My heart raced. Before I could gather my thoughts, the tears started to fall. I didn't expect the trigger. I didn't expect the wave of grief to come crashing back in like that, decades later. But that's the thing about trauma—it lives in your body, and it doesn't always ask permission before it rises.

And just like that, I was back in the waiting room.

Waiting rooms are more than just spaces with chairs and magazines. They are places of anxiety, of anticipation, of surrender. You sit. You wonder. You hope. You fear.

I've waited in so many—medical waiting rooms, emotional ones, spiritual ones. But the longest waiting room I've ever known is the one life put me in that day at Grady. It became the setting for every other season of waiting.

At four years old, I waited for my name to be called and for someone to tell me I'd be okay. As a teen, I waited for the kind of love I read about in books—something gentle, something safe. As a young woman, I waited to walk down the aisle, thinking marriage would end the waiting. But even then, I found myself waiting in silence, waiting for respect, for kindness, for my husband to come home.

I waited to feel like enough.

I waited for motherhood to fulfill the void in me, only to realize I had unknowingly transferred my waiting onto my children. They sat in the waiting room with me—waiting for affection, for attention, for healing I hadn't yet found myself.

And still, God was there.

Every time I thought the waiting room would break me, it became a classroom.

At some point, I stopped asking, "Why me?" and started asking, "What now, Lord?"

I realized the waiting room wasn't a punishment. It was a preparation. God wasn't ignoring me—He was refining me. He was stripping away everything I thought I needed so I could see that all I ever needed was Him.

I came to understand that the world defines waiting as delay and denial, but in the Word of God, waiting is sacred. It's where hope is planted. It's where faith is tested. It's where transformation begins.

The Hebrew word for "wait" carries the connotation of anticipation and hope—not helplessness. And the Bible is full of those who waited: Abraham waited for a son, Joseph waited in prison, Hannah waited for a child, David waited for his throne, and even Jesus waited in the garden before the cross.

I'm in good company.

Waiting hurts, yes. But it also reveals what's really in your heart. It exposes your trust issues, your control issues, your faith issues. And sometimes, it reveals that what you've been praying for isn't what you *need*—what you need is to let go and trust God's timing.

I've learned that waiting doesn't always end the way you think it will. Sometimes the healing comes, sometimes it doesn't. Sometimes the marriage is restored, sometimes it ends. Sometimes you get the job, the call, the answer—and sometimes, all you get is peace. But peace is enough.

Because God is enough.

He has never forgotten me in the waiting room. He sits beside me while the minutes stretch into months and the prayers turn into tears. He holds me when the silence is too loud. He sends reminders—through songs, through scripture, through people—just when I think I can't sit there a moment longer.

One day, I heard a song by Tasha Cobbs called "Why Not Me?" It was like someone had reached into my heart and put my pain into melody. The lyrics ministered to me in a way I didn't expect. That song reminded me that maybe I was chosen for this—this pain, this journey, this platform—because God knew I could carry it, and more importantly, that I wouldn't carry it alone.

Yes, the waiting room gets lonely. People forget you're there. Life goes on for others while you sit still. And yet, God always knows where to find you.

He knows your name.

He calls it—not just in the doctor's office, but in the quiet places where your soul feels like it's slipping.

There were days I wondered if I'd ever stop waiting—waiting for a cure, for a diagnosis, for a break. But now I understand: I may never leave the medical waiting room. And that's okay. Because I've learned how to wait well. I've learned to wait with praise on my lips and peace in my heart. I've learned to wait with intention, to serve while waiting, to encourage while waiting, to write while waiting.

Waiting taught me how to worship.

Chapter 4
Grief Times Two + One

*The Lord is near to those who have a broken heart
And saves such as have a contrite spirit.
– Psalm 34:18 (NKJV)*

2009 is a year tattooed on my soul.

It was the year the ground beneath me gave way—the year my life split open and grief became my shadow. It was the year I lost the two women who anchored my life—my grandmother and my mother—just seventeen days apart.

And though the years have rolled forward, though I've learned to speak their names without tears choking my voice, there are still days when I feel the ache like it's brand new. Because when you lose your roots, your branches sway in a different kind of wind.

My grandmother was turning 75 that spring, and I wanted to do something special. Not just for her, but for me. I needed her to know just how deeply she was loved—not just as our matriarch, but as the woman who held us all together. So I planned a surprise birthday celebration. I designed the flyer myself, coordinated the guest list, and asked every adult in the family to contribute. Not everyone did. Most didn't, if I'm being honest. But I didn't let it stop me. I covered the costs because I believed she was worth it.

And it was beautiful.

Her sisters came. Her oldest friends came—some traveled from far away just to surprise her. All five of her children were there. Her twelve grandchildren. Her great-grandbabies running around the tables. We presented her with tributes from each generation, and I watched her face light up with joy, with pride, with gratitude. That night was filled with love, even if I was quietly frustrated that the financial burden had fallen mostly on me.

I didn't know that would be the last time we'd all be together under the same roof.

The next weekend was Easter. A family tradition. Every year, we gathered at her house after church for Sunday dinner. But that year, I was still a little salty. Still feeling unappreciated. So when my grandmother called on Good Friday to invite me, I said no.

Minutes later, my aunt called me too. "Please reconsider," she said. There was something in her voice—a gentle insistence I couldn't ignore. So I agreed. I told her I'd bring my kids and stop by.

What I didn't know until later was that the invitation wasn't for the whole family. It was just for me and my children.

When I walked into her home that Easter Sunday, the table was already set. My grandmother had prepared a feast—and not just any feast. She had made my favorites: sweet tea mixed with lemonade (what some call an Arnold Palmer) and German Chocolate Pound Cake with coconut and cherries. It was her signature. It was my weakness. And it was love, baked into every bite. She even had a delicious baked ham on a beautiful crystal platter.

We sat at the kitchen table together, just the two of us, talking. Laughing. Catching up. She handed me a thank you card with $50 inside—her way of expressing gratitude for the party. That's the kind of woman she was. Thoughtful. Quietly generous. Intentional.

I had no idea that would be the last meal I'd ever eat from her hands.

If I had known, I would have lingered longer. I would've told her everything—how much she meant to me, how her faith shaped mine, how her strength carried generations. I would have hugged her a little tighter, soaked in her scent a little deeper, memorized the sound of her voice just a bit more intentionally.

Two days later, she was gone.

I got the call and rushed to Emory Midtown—what we used to call Crawford Long. My heart pounded as I drove, trying to get there in time. My best friend Caryn stayed on the phone with me as I raced down the highway. Then my aunt called. "Come to the family room," she said.

The family room.

I knew what that meant.

I didn't want to know, but I knew.

When I arrived, I met my aunt at the emergency room entrance. The news had already been delivered: my grandmother had died of a massive heart attack.

Just like that.
Gone.

It felt unreal—like a cruel joke. Just days before, she had cooked, laughed, poured me tea. And now I was standing outside of time, clutching my chest, trying to breathe.

We returned to her house after leaving the hospital. And there, in the quiet of her kitchen, was the cake she had baked for me. Still wrapped. Still untouched. Her last gift to me, waiting like she knew I'd need something sweet to soften the bitterness of loss.

As I pulled the leftovers from the fridge for my family, I had barely grabbed the crystal platter when it slipped out of my hands and shattered across the kitchen floor. The sound pierced the silence. The platter, just like my heart, was broken. All I could do was cry as my uncle cleaned up the pieces and tried to comfort me. We were all numb.

Everyone ate whatever they could find in the fridge—she had cooked enough for an army. But the cake? That was mine. And I didn't share it.

Planning her funeral felt like walking through water with bricks tied to my ankles. I had never done a funeral program before, but my family asked—and I said yes. They asked me to sing. I said yes. I didn't question. I didn't pause. I just did it. Because that's what you do when love is bigger than your grief.

Her service was beautiful. Everything she had asked for in her final wishes—horse-drawn carriage, white doves, elegance. Her goodbye was fit for a queen.

I didn't know I'd be planning another one less than three weeks later.

Thirteen days after we laid my grandmother to rest, my mother—the woman who birthed me, who waited with me in hospital rooms, who stood beside me when the world didn't—was gone too.

Another massive heart attack. Another trip down the highway but this time to a different hospital. Another family room.

But this time... it was my mother.

My grief shifted. It hit differently. Losing my grandmother broke my heart. Losing my mother broke my soul.

This death wasn't planned. There were no final wishes. No insurance policy. Just confusion, chaos, and pain. I remembered her once mentioning cremation. So that's what we did. And again, I did what was asked of me—I created the program. I sang. I held my emotions long enough to get through the service. And then I collapsed in private.

Two funerals in seventeen days.
Two queens.
Gone.

And me?
I was still expected to show up, be strong, keep going. But I was drowning in sorrow, and no one seemed to notice.

There were many phone calls, cards, and thoughts of encouragement, but a lot of people really didn't know what to say. I understood that—because I didn't know what to say either. Several people from church brought food. One sweet lady brought a cake on a beautiful crystal platter.

Days later, I stood at my kitchen sink, washing that same platter. My hands were wet, my mind far away, when it slipped. I watched it crash to the floor, shattering into a thousand pieces—just like the one in my grandmother's kitchen sixteen days earlier. Two losses. Two broken platters. The sound was the same, but this time, it stole my breath.

Both times, my heart was already fractured. But this time, I couldn't breathe.

Sixteen years later, I can finally talk about it without tears. But I still feel it. I still miss them. I still wonder what life would be like if they were here.

And just when I thought I had learned to carry the weight of those two losses, another one came.

+ One

Caryn.

My best friend. My sister in spirit. The one who walked through those losses with me, who sat in those waiting rooms beside me. The one who answered the phone that day when I called in a panic, driving to the hospital. The one who comforted me through my grandmother's death and my mother's memorial service.

We met when I was 14 and she was 15. High school friends turned lifetime soulmates. We did everything together—celebrated victories, held space for heartbreaks, and even got baptized together in 2008. We obeyed the gospel side-by-side, committing our lives to Christ in the same water. Our friendship spanned four decades. She stood with me through my divorce. I stood with her when her husband passed.

And now I'm writing this chapter with a different kind of ache—because Caryn passed away on Monday, July 28, 2025.

- One.

Grief again.

Another hole in my heart.

She battled Lupus with the same grace and grit she brought to everything. Her passing feels like another fracture in my foundation—but I take comfort in knowing she is no longer suffering. Her fight is over. Her faith has become sight.

Grief is not linear. It's not something you graduate from. It lives in layers, surfacing when you least expect it. Some days, it whispers. Some days, it screams.

But what I've learned is this: the strength to endure grief doesn't come from willpower. It comes from God.

He is close to the brokenhearted. He binds wounds the world cannot see. He whispers hope into the hollow places and reminds us that death is not the end for those who believe.

Chapter 5
The Strength of a Limp

"Just as he crossed over Penuel the sun rose on him, and he limped on his hip."
-Genesis 32:31 (NKJV)

There's a certain kind of strength that only reveals itself when you realize you can't run anymore—but you choose to keep moving anyway.

It's the strength of a limp.

Not the kind that people applaud, but the kind that speaks volumes in silence. The kind that says, *"Yes, I'm still hurting. But no, I'm not giving up."*

That's been my walk for quite some time now. And though my physical limitations were born from a childhood trauma I didn't choose, the spiritual journey of walking with a limp has taught me more than a life of ease ever could.

I used to believe that healing meant full restoration—walking without pain, living without pause, breathing without the weight of memories. But I've since learned that healing sometimes looks like limping. And even in the limp, there is purpose.

I've spent years trying to walk "normal." Trying to keep pace with a world that moves too fast and leaves no room for pause. I've forced smiles through searing pain, both in my body and in my soul. And for a long time, I thought I had to prove that I was strong.

But strength doesn't always roar.

Sometimes it limps.
Sometimes it leans.
Sometimes it whispers, "Lord, just help me take one more step."

And He always does.

Getting out of my own way has been one of the hardest lessons of my life.

I've spent so many years showing up for everyone else—being the dependable one, the strong one, the helper, the fixer. But I often left myself out of the equation. Somewhere between raising children, helping others, building a business, and carrying my own pain, I forgot to ask God what He wanted for *me*.

It wasn't until my children grew up that I started hearing the silence.

No more homework.
No more school drop-offs or late-night dinners.
No more schedules revolving around other people's plans.
Just... silence.

And it was in that silence that God began to speak. Not in thunder. Not in chaos. But in stillness.

The dynamics of my life shifted when my children became adults.

In many ways, they became my motivation—my reason to push through. I wanted to be better *for* them. But now that they are living their own lives, I had to confront the question: *Who am I when no one needs me?*

It was a hard truth to sit with.

There were moments I felt lost. Moments when the pain in my body mirrored the ache in my heart. I missed the noise. I missed the routine. I missed the purpose I had grown so used to. But it was in this new space that God invited me to go deeper—not in performance, but in presence.

He reminded me that purpose evolves.

Just because one season ends doesn't mean my usefulness ends with it.

So I turned my eyes back to the calling He placed in me long ago: to serve, to mentor, to lead with compassion. To help parents help their children make better choices. To help youth believe that their story matters—before the world tries to convince them otherwise.

That calling never left. It just matured.

My own pain gave birth to my passion.

I understood what it felt like to be unseen, unheard, and unprotected. And I never wanted a child to feel that way. That's why I poured myself into my mentoring programs—not because I had all the answers, but because I remembered what it felt like to have none.

I created safe spaces for children and teens to talk, write, reflect, and be vulnerable. I helped parents rediscover their children—not just their behavior, but their hearts. I taught them that parenting isn't about control; it's about connection. And I did it all while limping.

There were days when I walked into schools or community centers with tears behind my eyes and pain in my joints. But the moment I saw a young person light up because someone believed in them, the ache was worth it.

Because *this* is what limping toward the light looks like—it's not about perfection, it's about progress.

I still wrestle with pain—both emotional and physical. There are mornings when my body doesn't want to move. When getting out of bed feels like a negotiation. When everything in me wants to give up.

But then I remember Jacob.

In the Bible, Jacob wrestled with an angel all night long. And when the sun came up, he walked away with a limp—but also with a blessing. His name was changed. His destiny was affirmed. His limp wasn't a punishment—it was a mark of encounter.

That story changed me.

Because like Jacob, I've wrestled. I've cried out to God in the midnight hours. I've asked "why" more times than I can count. And though I didn't always get answers, I always got *grace.*

I walk with a limp, yes. But I also walk with power. With favor. With purpose. Because in my weakness, His strength is made perfect.

Let me be honest.

There were moments I questioned if I was still valuable. When your pace slows, people start to move on without you. When your pain becomes a regular part of your life, others forget that it's still there. I've had to battle against the lie that says, "You're not doing enough."

But God reminds me daily: *"You are enough, because I am enough in you."*

And that's when I began to surrender—not just my pain, but my plans.

I stopped trying to fit into boxes that no longer served me.
I stopped chasing validation from people who couldn't see the fullness of my heart.

I stopped hiding my limp.
And I started walking with it—toward the light.

That light? It's not always bright.

Sometimes it's a flicker in the distance. Sometimes it's barely visible through the fog. But it's there. Always. Leading me. Guiding me. Reminding me that I'm never walking alone.

The older I get, the more I understand that walking with God doesn't mean the path will be smooth. It means the presence will be constant.

And that's enough for me.

I've come to cherish the stillness of this new season.

Without the daily demands of raising children, I've had space to reflect, to write, to pour into others in new ways. I've hosted workshops. I've created curriculum. I've coached parents. I've helped children find their voices and use them to rewrite their stories.

I've mentored from my scars—not my perfection. And that authenticity has opened doors no resume ever could.

And I've discovered something beautiful: the more I give, the more God gives back. Not always in money. Not always in recognition. But in peace. In joy. In impact.

That's wealth to me.

I'm still limping, yes.

But my limp is no longer a symbol of what's broken. It's a reminder of what I've survived. It's a testimony in motion.

Every step I take, every story I help bring to life, every young person I encourage—it all testifies to a God who brings beauty from ashes, purpose from pain, and strength from suffering.

And so I keep walking.

Chapter 6
When God Changes the Prescription

For I know the thoughts that I think toward you, says the Lord, thoughts of peace and not of evil, to give you a future and a hope.
—Jeremiah 29:11 (NKJV)

There are moments in life that never leave you. Not because they were dramatic or loud, but because they marked a shift—an internal turning point where the old way of thinking crumbled and something deeper took its place.

For me, one of those moments came on February 20, 2020.

It was my fourth trip to the Mayo Clinic in just four months. By that point, I had grown familiar with the cold examination tables, the maze of hallways, the endless lab work, and the polite but concerned expressions of doctors who didn't have clear answers. I knew how to pack for the week, what snacks to bring, and which veins were still "somewhat" good for blood draws. I was tired, in pain, and more emotionally worn than I cared to admit.

I sat on the edge of the exam table, my legs dangling as if I were still that little girl from long ago—unsure, hurting, and hoping someone could fix what was broken. The doctor came in, reviewed my chart, examined me, then looked me in the eyes with the kind of honesty that leaves no room for false hope.

He said, *"While you are not dying, you are suffering."*

The words landed like a weighted blanket—heavy, suffocating, undeniable. At that moment, I knew. I knew that what was going on in my body—the fatigue, the inflammation, the chronic pain—wasn't going to kill me, but it was going to be with me. It wasn't fatal, but it was debilitating. It wasn't terminal, but it was tormenting.

And that's when God started changing the prescription.

Up until that moment, I had been chasing healing the way the world defines it—complete restoration, no more pain, full strength, and a return to "normal." But what the doctor's words made me realize is that God had something else in mind. Healing, in His hands, doesn't always look like the removal of pain. Sometimes, it looks like the presence of peace *in* the pain.

As fear tried to crawl into my mind, courage rose in my spirit. It didn't shout. It didn't demand. It simply stood up—quiet and firm—and reminded me of who walks with me. Because courage isn't the absence of fear. It's the choice to move forward in spite of it. And in that exam room, I chose courage.

More than five years have passed, and I can still hear those words. They echo in the chambers of my soul, not as a sentence, but as a summons—a call to live not just with my condition but through it. To walk in purpose even when the pain is ever-present. To find strength not in the absence of struggle but in the nearness of God.

The truth is, we live in a world that's in constant turmoil. And if we're honest, sometimes even believers get tired. Sometimes we find ourselves facing battles that feel too big, too long, too exhausting. We're told to have faith, but we're also human. We have moments when our knees buckle and our hearts question, "God, how much more?"

But courage—real, raw courage—isn't about having all the answers. It's about choosing to trust God even when we don't understand the assignment. It's about standing on the promises of God even when the ground beneath us feels unstable.

The dictionary defines courage as "the mental or moral strength to venture, persevere, and withstand danger, fear, or difficulty." It doesn't promise ease—it calls for endurance. It doesn't deny fear—it just chooses to fight anyway.

I've cried more nights than I can count. I've held my pillow tight, pleading for the pain to stop. I've asked God the hard questions. I've felt unseen, unheard, and undone.

And still, I rise.

Because while my diagnosis didn't change, my *definition* of healing did.

Letting go of what I thought healing should look like was a painful but necessary surrender. I had to release my own expectations—my "if only" prayers, my assumptions about how God should fix me, my longing for a life without limitations.

God wasn't asking me to stop believing for better. He was asking me to start trusting Him for *different*.

Different isn't always less. Sometimes different is deeper.

He changed the prescription—from removal to reliance. From rescue to resilience. From cure to courage.

And I had to decide: would I hold onto my version of healing and stay stuck in disappointment? Or would I embrace His version and walk forward, even if I had to limp?

Yes, life has handed me lemons. Big ones. Bitter ones. And I've thrown myself more than a few pity parties. I've murmured. I've complained. I've had days when I didn't want to get out of bed—when the weight of chronic illness felt like too much to bear.

But when I take a step back and truly reflect, I see it clearly: God has still been so very good to me.

Even in the valley, He's been faithful. Even in the waiting room, He's been present. Even in the suffering, He's been sustaining me with a grace I can't explain.

I don't know what the future holds. I never did. But I know this: if I can trust God through the hard days, I'll appreciate the easy days so much more. If I can thank Him while limping, I'll praise Him even more when I'm dancing.

I know that if I remember His promises—persistent, powerful, and peaceful—I will courageously endure by the light of His love.

Encouragement is oxygen to the soul. We all need it. We all crave it. Whether we're battling illness, loss, fear, or uncertainty, we need someone to remind us that we are not alone, that we are still valuable, that our story still matters.

That's why I keep sharing.

Because somebody needs to know that suffering doesn't mean forgotten. That a chronic condition doesn't disqualify you from divine calling. That God isn't finished just because life took an unexpected turn.

When God changes the prescription, it's not because He's withholding healing—it's because He's offering something even more eternal. Healing that reaches beyond the body and touches the soul. Healing that teaches us to worship in the wilderness. Healing that helps us see beyond the pain and into the purpose.

I've learned to find Him in the stillness. To hear Him in the silence. To trust Him in the detour.

And when I look at my life—the way I've been able to encourage others, to help parents, to mentor youth, to build Pa-Pro-Vi Publishing into a platform for healing—I can't help but see the blessing in the brokenness.

Because that's what God does. He takes what hurts and turns it into hope. He takes what was meant to break us and uses it to build us.

So here I am. Still walking. Still working. Still waiting some days. Still wounded on others.

But never without courage.

Never without grace.

And never without purpose.

Because when God changes the prescription, He also strengthens the patient.

Chapter 7
The Birth of Pa-Pro-Vi Publisher

And we know that all things work together for good to those who love God, to those who are called according to His purpose – Romans 8:28 (NKJV)

I never intended to start a publishing company.

I never set out to become a writing coach or to help people around the world share their stories. There was no formal business plan or carefully crafted marketing strategy. There was just a hospital room, a worn-out body, a weary soul—and a whisper from God that said, *"This pain has a purpose."*

Pa-Pro-Vi Publishing was not born in a conference room or from a spark of ambition. It was born in a place of suffering. A place of surrender. A place where I had nothing left but faith.

And that was more than enough.

I was still in recovery—physically, mentally, and emotionally—when the vision for Pa-Pro-Vi began to take shape. It was late 2019, and I had just begun a series of medical visits to the Mayo Clinic in Jacksonville, Florida. My health had once again taken a turn. I had grown used to the cycle by then: pain, doctors, tests, no answers. But something about this season felt different. Heavier. More layered.

By February 2020, on my fourth trip in four months, the doctor finally looked me in the eyes and said the words that would reroute the course of my life: *"While you are not dying, you are suffering."*

It wasn't the worst news I had ever heard. But it was definitive. It let me know that the pain I was experiencing had no cure. That this chronic battle was not going to disappear overnight—or maybe not ever.

I could feel the fear trying to creep in, wrapping itself around my mind like ivy. The kind of fear that makes you question if life is always going to feel this hard. But before the fear could fully settle, something else stood up within me: *courage.*

It was around that same time that I got a call from an old high school classmate. We hadn't talked in years, but she remembered that I had written a book— *Walking Limitations by Other People's Definition.*

She told me she had a story too, but didn't know where to begin.

"I need your help," she said.

I could have easily told her no. I was away from home, dealing with a fresh diagnosis, and trying to wrap my mind around what the rest of my life might look like. But something in her voice stirred something in me. Something I hadn't felt in a while.

Purpose.

So I helped her. Step by step, word by word. I walked her through what I had done to bring my story to life. I gave her the roadmap I never had. And somewhere in between the coaching calls and the manuscript drafts, something unexpected happened: *I felt alive again.*

Helping her tell her story reminded me why I told mine.

It was in that hotel room in Jacksonville, still aching from medical tests and still uncertain about what was happening in my body, that Pa-Pro-Vi Publishing was born. At the time, I didn't even know what to call it. I just knew that what I had given her, I needed to give to others. And not just for them—but for me.

Because in helping others write through their pain, I was healing through mine.

The name *Pa-Pro-Vi* came later. Pain. Progress. Victory.

It seemed so simple, but it held everything. My entire life story was wrapped up in those three words.

Pain—not just physical, but emotional, spiritual, generational. The kind of pain that doesn't always have a name but leaves a mark.

Progress—the slow, steady movement from who I was to who I was becoming. Sometimes messy, sometimes halting, but always forward.

Victory—not in the absence of struggle, but in the decision to keep going anyway. To rise. To write. To redeem the story.

Pa-Pro-Vi became my ministry before I even realized it was a business.

In the beginning, I didn't have much—just a laptop, a few contacts, and a story. But what I had more than anything was conviction. I knew what it felt like to sit with a story inside of you, unsure of how to release it. I knew the weight of silence. I knew the power of a well-told truth.

So I made a vow: I would help people take their stories from a *thought to a realization.*

No matter their background.
No matter their writing level.
No matter how painful the story was.

If they had a voice, I would help them use it. If they didn't have a voice, I'd help them find it.

Since 2020, Pa-Pro-Vi Publishing has helped bring over 150 solo book projects to life. That includes nearly 20 children's books and more than 20 anthologies, with dozens more in the works. I've coached over 450 authors—mothers, fathers, teachers, ministers, veterans, survivors, children, and elders. Some never imagined they'd write a book. Some had waited decades. But all of them had something to say.

Every story that comes through Pa-Pro-Vi is handled with care because I know how sacred it is to trust someone with your truth. We don't just edit—we *encourage.* We don't just format—we *foster faith.* We don't just publish—we *partner in purpose.*

There is no "cookie cutter" at Pa-Pro-Vi. Each story is unique, and so is each journey.

I've had the honor of helping men who were formerly incarcerated write redemption stories. I've guided women through the process of releasing generational trauma. I've walked with children as they wrote about bullying, autism, courage, and faith. I've helped pastors, poets, and everyday people bring healing to others by first healing themselves.

We've created anthologies like *Our Journey from Boys to Men, Our Journey from Girls to Women,* and *Ouch! Lies Hurt*—books that do more than sit on a shelf. They sit in hearts. They ignite conversations. They start movements.

And none of it would have happened if I hadn't said yes.

But it hasn't always been easy.

Running a publishing business with a chronic condition is not for the faint of heart. There have been days when I've had to coach authors while fighting through pain that made it hard to sit upright. There have been nights when I've cried over deadlines, not because I couldn't meet them—but because my body was begging me to rest.

And there were moments I doubted myself. Moments I wondered if I was qualified. Moments I heard the enemy whisper, *"Who do you think you are?"*

But then God would send a reminder.

An email from an author saying, "This changed my life."
A reader message that said, "This book gave me the courage to forgive."
A child holding their first published book and saying, "I'm an author now."

And I'd remember: this is bigger than me.

Pa-Pro-Vi Publishing isn't just a company.

It's a *calling*.

It's a place where broken people become brave people.
Where trauma becomes testimony.
Where silence becomes sound.
Where survival becomes storytelling.

We are a storytelling ministry, and books are our altar.

More than publishing, we've also expanded into mentorship. I've led youth creative writing programs to help children process their emotions through stories. I've created curriculum for schools and churches. I've guided parents in helping their children make better choices through writing, reflection, and truth-telling.

Because I believe when we teach the next generation how to use their voice, we give them the power to shape their own narrative—and stop repeating ours.

Through Pa-Pro-Vi, I've spoken on panels, hosted summits, facilitated coaching programs, and created spaces for healing that I wish I had when I was younger.

It's not just about books. It's about breakthrough.

Today, Pa-Pro-Vi continues to grow. Our authors have become international bestsellers. Our anthologies have started healing conversations in homes, schools, prisons, and churches. We've built a legacy, and we're just getting started.

And I owe it all to the Great Publisher—the Author and Finisher of my faith.

He took a patient, and turned her into a publisher.
He took my limp, and turned it into leadership.
He took my pain, and turned it into platform.

And I'm still saying yes.

Chapter 8
The Ministry of Storytelling

And they overcame him by the blood of the Lamb and by the word of their testimony, and they did not love their lives to the death. – Revelation 12:11 (NKJV)

I used to think ministry had to happen behind a pulpit.

That it required a robe, a title, or a microphone. That God's work looked like sermons preached on Sunday morning, not quiet conversations held across Zoom screens, late-night editing sessions, or the sacred exchange that happens when someone says, "I'm ready to tell my truth."

But somewhere between my pain and my purpose, I discovered something different.

I discovered that **storytelling is a ministry**—a holy space where healing flows, chains break, and testimonies are written in ink instead of shame. I discovered that every book I've helped bring into the world was not just a product. It was a *process*—for the author, and for me.

Because as I've helped authors take their stories from a thought to a realization, they've helped me heal in ways I didn't even know I still needed.

When I first launched Pa-Pro-Vi Publishing, I had no idea it would become a healing center disguised as a publishing house. I thought I was just helping people publish books. I didn't realize I was stepping into a deeper calling—*a ministry of mending broken places through storytelling.*

Time and time again, I've witnessed what happens when someone gives themselves permission to be honest. When they pick up the pen and face the thing they've been running from. When they write down the words that once stole their voice and reclaim their power by speaking them out loud.

That's ministry.

There was a woman I worked with early on. She came to me unsure, timid, and filled with doubt. Her story was layered with abuse, abandonment, and the kind of betrayal that leaves permanent scars. She said, "I'm not a writer." I smiled and said, "You're a survivor. And that's more than enough."

We met weekly. Chapter by chapter, she opened up. Sometimes she cried more than she wrote. Sometimes she needed permission to rest. But she kept showing up. And when the day came for her to hold her finished book in her hands, she wept. "I didn't think I could do this," she said. "But now that I have, I feel free."

And I understood. Because I felt free too.

Each author that comes through Pa-Pro-Vi brings a piece of my own healing with them. Every story they share gives me permission to go deeper in my own. Every "aha" moment they experience becomes an echo of something God is still doing in me.

There was the veteran who had never spoken a word about what he saw overseas. Decades of silence wrapped in military structure and masculine pride. But once he began writing, it all came pouring out— the fear, the loss, the anger. His story became not just a book, but a bridge—to his family, to his healing, and to others who thought they had to suffer alone.

Another author had survived childhood sexual abuse but had never told a soul. She said, "I don't want to die with this in me." So she wrote. Gently. Bravely. Bit by bit. By the end, she told me, "This was the first time I've felt seen. Not just by others—but by myself."

That's when I knew this was more than publishing. This was resurrection.
Not of the dead—but of the silenced.

Storytelling is sacred because it requires vulnerability. It asks you to revisit moments that nearly broke you. To sit with the discomfort. To look at your younger self with compassion. To name the thing that once held power over you—and in doing so, *take that power back.*

I've worked with women who've lost children, men who've battled addiction, teens who've been bullied, and elders who waited a lifetime to tell their truth. And through every one of them, I've seen the hand of God at work—softening hearts, mending wounds, transforming shame into strength.

But it's not just their healing. It's mine too.

There was a time I believed I had to hide my own pain to help others. That I had to be polished and perfect to be effective. But what I've learned through this ministry is that *people don't need your perfection—they need your presence.* They need to know you've been there too. That you're still walking through it. That your limp is not a liability—it's a light.

Helping others tell their stories reminds me every day that I'm still writing mine.

And sometimes, their stories hold keys to parts of me I didn't even know were locked.

I remember a young girl—just nineteen—who wanted to write a book about what caregivers go through when they are working with someone living with autism. Her words were simple, but her spirit was pure. She said, "I want people to know that different isn't bad. It's just different." That project taught me to see people not by their labels, but by their light.

There's the man who wanted to write about the abuse and abandonment he experienced for his mother and father. He didn't want to shame them, he just wanted to understand. And through his story, he found healing—and is now able to share his story with others in the same situation.

That's the beauty of storytelling—it doesn't just free the writer. It frees the reader too.

Over the years, I've facilitated anthologies that brought together hundreds of voices. Some of these people never imagined they'd write a book, let alone become bestselling authors. But when they said yes to sharing, a door was unlocked.

They wrote about surviving domestic violence.
About overcoming depression.
About rediscovering themselves after divorce.
About raising children with special needs.
About finding God in the middle of grief.

And as they wrote, walls came down.
And as they spoke, chains broke.
And as they published, people were delivered.

Every anthology we've done has had one goal: *to remind people that they're not alone.* That their pain is not in vain. That their voice matters.

Because sometimes, all it takes to change a life is one sentence. One story. One honest, unfiltered, grace-soaked truth.

People often ask me what makes Pa-Pro-Vi Publishing different.

My answer is simple: we don't just publish books.
We *minister through manuscripts.*
We *pray over paragraphs.*
We *coach with compassion.*
We *love through the editing.*

Because for many of our authors, this isn't just a creative journey—it's a spiritual one.

And I don't take that lightly.

The truth is, storytelling healed me first.

Writing *Walking Limitations by Other People's Definition* cracked something open in me. It was my first public confession. The moment I stopped hiding and started healing. That book wasn't a product—it was a lifeline.

And now, I get to help others find their lifeline too.

Each author I serve becomes part of my journey. Part of my healing. Part of my testimony.

Their courage reminds me to be courageous.
Their breakthroughs remind me to keep going.
Their stories remind me that this work is worth it—even on the hard days.

I've learned that ministry doesn't have to be loud. Sometimes it whispers. Sometimes it weeps. Sometimes it looks like a virtual coaching call with a woman crying into her keyboard, and me saying, "Take your time. We'll write through it together."

Sometimes it looks like a child grinning ear to ear, holding their first book like it's treasure.
Sometimes it's the sigh of relief that comes when someone finishes the last chapter of the story they swore they'd never be brave enough to tell.

And sometimes, it's just being still with someone in their truth—no fixing, no judging—just holding space.

That is ministry.
That is Pa-Pro-Vi.
That is me.

There is healing in sharing.

There is deliverance in declaring.

There is purpose in publishing.

And I count it an honor to be chosen for this work.

Every author that walks through our doors leaves an imprint on my heart. They are not just clients—they are co-laborers in the ministry of truth. Together, we are reclaiming the narrative. Resurrecting voices. And restoring what was stolen.

Chapter 9
From Thought to Realization

"Write the vision and make it plain..."
– Habakkuk 2:2 (KJV)

When people ask me to explain what *Pa-Pro-Vi Publishing* is, I tell them it's not just a business—it's a *birthing place*. A sacred space where stories come to life. A ministry where thoughts are transformed into healing. A journey that begins with a whisper in someone's spirit and ends with a book in their hands—a testimony in print.

We turn thoughts into realizations.
That is the mission.
That is the call.
That is the assignment.

And it was birthed not from confidence, but from brokenness.

The phrase *"From Thought to Realization"* didn't come to me overnight. It came through experience. Through years of holding other people's pain.

Through moments when I sat across from someone who didn't think their story mattered and reminded them, "Not only does your story matter—someone's healing is waiting on it."

I didn't always have the language for it. But deep down, I always knew: every story has an audience. Every testimony has a purpose. And every struggle—when surrendered—has the potential to become someone else's survival guide.

I learned this because it happened to me.

When I wrote *Walking Limitations by Other People's Definition*, I wasn't thinking about bestselling lists or branding. I was trying to survive. I was writing my way out of pain. I was telling my story before it consumed me. And when people started responding—when they said, "I see myself in your journey," I realized that our stories don't just belong to us.

They're meant to be *given away*—so others can find themselves in the pages and realize they're not alone.

The idea of "From Thought to Realization" grew as I began coaching others through their writing. I watched the transformation happen every time. It always began the same way: a timid voice, a hesitant spirit, someone saying, "I don't know where to start."

And then the shift.

That first chapter.
That first cry.
That first moment of truth.

Something clicks. And the thought becomes a seed. And with nurturing, coaching, love, and accountability, that seed becomes a *realized* story—a finished manuscript, a printed book, a testimony ready to impact others.

I've seen it over and over again.

A thought that once seemed too hard to write becomes a story someone holds in their hands and says, "I did it."

That's what we do at Pa-Pro-Vi.
We help people go from *I think I want to…* to *I actually did it*.
From *Maybe one day…* to *Today is the day*.

But if I'm being honest, not everyone believed I could do this.

When I started Pa-Pro-Vi, there were people—some close to me—who questioned my ability. They looked at my physical limitations and assumed they disqualified me. I was hurt when someone I considered a friend asked me "What qualifies you?" They couldn't understand how someone who walked with a limp, who was in and out of the hospital, could run a publishing company. They didn't see the vision—because they didn't *have* the vision.

But God did.

And He gave it to me.

So I had to learn how to encourage myself. I had to learn how to believe in what God had whispered to me, even when the people around me couldn't see it.

I had to remind myself of what I already knew in my spirit:
That God doesn't call the qualified—He qualifies the called.
That He specializes in using the unlikely.
That He takes the very things others count out, and builds something undeniable.

There were nights I cried because I felt unsupported.
There were days I doubted myself because the enemy tried to convince me I wasn't enough.
There were times I considered giving up because I felt alone.

But then I'd remember the authors.
I'd remember the stories.
I'd remember the mission.

And I'd get back up. Limping, yes. But moving forward.

Because someone was waiting.

That's the truth that keeps me going—*someone is always waiting at the end of our stories.*

Waiting for a word that will break their silence.
Waiting for a story that mirrors their own.
Waiting for courage to show up in the form of someone else's transparency.

And if we stay silent, they stay stuck.

I realized early on that my obedience wasn't just about me—it was about *them*.

The woman in her 60s who had never told anyone about the abuse she experienced as a child.
The young man who thought his prison sentence was the end, until he discovered the power of redemption through writing.
The mother who lost her child and found solace by turning grief into a legacy on paper.

Each of them were waiting. And so many others still are.

That's why I keep writing.
That's why I keep publishing.
That's why I keep pushing others to share their truth—even when it's hard.

Because their healing is connected to their honesty. And someone else's healing is connected to their courage.

Helping others go from thought to realization has become my ministry.

It's not about grammar.
It's not about perfect punctuation.
It's not about whether the writer has a degree or knows the technical rules.

It's about *truth*.
It's about *testimony*.
It's about letting God get glory through a story once buried in shame.

And every time someone trusts me with their story, I don't take it lightly. Because I remember what it was like to be on the other side—nervous, uncertain, wondering if anyone would care.

I care. Because I've been there.

And I know what happens when someone finally says, "I'm ready."

There's a shift that takes place when a person realizes their story is *not too messy, not too small, and not too late.* That moment is powerful. And it always reminds me of the moment I had to make that decision for myself.

No one handed me a blueprint.
No one gave me permission.
No one offered guarantees.

But I wrote anyway.
I shared anyway.
I published anyway.

Because I knew that if God gave me the story, He would give me the strength.

And now I help others tap into that same strength.

Some of the greatest miracles I've seen didn't happen in a church—they happened in a coaching call. They happened when someone broke down in the middle of writing a hard chapter and finally let themselves grieve. They happened when someone who had carried guilt for decades wrote their story and found release in the process. They happened when a child saw their name on the cover of a book and said, "I'm an author!"

These are not just books.

They're breakthroughs.

And I get to witness them every day.

So when I say we help people go from *thought to realization*, I don't just mean we help them publish books.

I mean we help them realize:

- That their voice matters.

- That their pain has purpose.
- That their story can bring healing—not just to others, but to themselves.

We help them realize that they are not what happened to them.
That they are not forgotten.
That they have something to say—and someone is waiting to hear it.

I'm often asked, "How do you keep going with everything you face physically?" My answer is simple: *This is bigger than me.*

When you understand that your assignment is divine, you stop waiting for perfect conditions to move. You move because God said so.

Every story I help birth reminds me that I am exactly where I'm supposed to be.

Yes, I walk with limitations.
Yes, I've been overlooked and underestimated.
Yes, I've had to clap for myself when no one else did.

But I've also seen what happens when people find their voice.

And that, to me, is worth everything.

Chapter 10
The Power of Collective Healing

"Being confident of this very thing, that He who began a good work in you will complete it until the day of Christ Jesus."
—Philippians 1:6 (NIV)

There's something indescribably beautiful about the sound of multiple voices rising at once—not in unison, but in harmony. That's what storytelling through anthologies has taught me. It's not always about saying the same thing or having lived the same experience. It's about the power of connection, the strength in shared vulnerability, and the healing that takes place when one person dares to speak up, and others realize they're not alone. That's the heartbeat of Pa-Pro-Vi Publishing's anthology projects. Each one has become a tapestry of triumph, stitched together by the brave hearts of those who said, "Yes, I will share."

Our first anthology, *I Did It, Teen Mom Success*, was born out of the need to rewrite a narrative that too many young women had been forced to believe.

"You're stuck," they said. "You've ruined your future," they whispered. Some even said, "You'll end up just like your mother." But I knew differently. I knew the power of resilience and the beauty of a determined soul. I gathered twelve women who had walked that road—not just survived teen pregnancy, but turned what was meant to be a limitation into liberation. They didn't stop when people turned their backs or when society labeled them. They prayed. They pivoted. They pressed forward.

These women had known homelessness, rejection, and abuse. They'd heard the voices of doubt—sometimes even from their own minds. But through it all, they rose. They held their babies and their dreams with equal strength. They didn't wait for permission to be successful. They gave themselves that permission, and with every word they wrote in that anthology, they gave it to other young girls too. The day *I Did It* launched, I remember reading the messages from readers who saw themselves in those pages. That's when I realized: collective healing isn't just possible—it's powerful.

Our Journey From Girls to Women was like looking into a mirror with a hundred different reflections. Each woman in that book had a story that started in the innocence of girlhood and walked through the fire of life into womanhood. Some carried trauma. Others carried silence. Many carried both. But all of them came to the table with courage. The stories of betrayal, abuse, rejection, and disappointment didn't just make us cry—they made us connect. They reminded us that becoming a woman isn't just about growing up—it's about growing through.

When I read the stories in that anthology, I thought about the little girl I once was—the one who limped not just physically, but emotionally. The girl who felt unseen, unheard, and misunderstood. Through these stories, I saw her begin to heal. And when we launched that book, I saw something else: women who had never met before holding hands, laughing through tears, and celebrating each other's transformation. Healing became communal. Testimonies became contagious.

And then came *Our Journey From Boys to Men*. That one hit differently. For so long, our culture has told boys to "man up," to suppress their feelings, and to walk in silence. This anthology gave them permission to speak. Over twenty men—from pastors to former hustlers—shared their journeys with unfiltered truth. They talked about fatherlessness, the pressure to provide, the confusion of manhood, and the pain of not knowing where to turn.

One of the authors wrote, "I didn't become a man when I turned 18. I became a man when I realized I could cry, ask for help, and still be strong." That stayed with me. Because strength isn't the absence of emotion—it's the courage to feel it and keep going anyway. I watched men find healing not just in writing their stories but in reading each other's. Some of them said it was the first time they ever said those words out loud. That's the power of collective storytelling. It doesn't just change the reader—it transforms the writer too.

Then came *The Women of the Waiting Room*. That project was spiritual in every sense of the word. It wasn't just about stories—it was about ministry. Thirty-three women opened up about the hardest seasons of their lives—times when they felt like God was silent, when they were stuck in the in-between, waiting on healing, on answers, on peace. Through poetry, testimonies, devotionals, and affirmations, they offered a lifeline to anyone sitting in their own "waiting room."

This book was a reflection of the spiritual healing I've experienced in my own waiting seasons. It reminded me that the waiting room isn't a punishment—it's preparation. And while we wait, we can worship. While we cry, we can still believe. I will never forget the launch event for *The Women of the Waiting Room*—women sat with tears in their eyes, saying "This book is my story too." And it was.

She Said Yes to Herself Unapologetically was a declaration more than a title. It was bold, vibrant, and full of fire. These were women who had once said yes to everyone else—yes to roles, to responsibilities, to people who drained them. But this time, they said yes to themselves. Yes to healing. Yes to boundaries. Yes to joy. Their stories reminded me that as women, we often carry the world on our shoulders. But we are allowed—no, we are commanded—to carry ourselves with love and intentionality.

One author wrote, "I said yes to myself and walked away from everything that hurt me—including my own negative self-talk." That's what this project was about. It wasn't selfish—it was sacred. Saying yes to ourselves is how we teach others to value us.

Addicted to Bliss took a different approach. It wasn't just about overcoming drugs or alcohol—it was about identifying the sneaky addictions we don't often talk about: overworking, people-pleasing, perfectionism, emotional numbing, and self-sabotage. These authors got real about the habits that kept them stuck and the radical joy they found when they chose healing.

This anthology was necessary because so many of us are addicted to pain—and we don't even know it. We run from bliss because we don't think we deserve it. But every story in that book said the same thing: you are worthy of happiness. You don't have to earn it. You just have to choose it.

And finally, *We Choose to Be More Than Our Diagnoses*. That book broke chains. Sixteen individuals with physical, emotional, and mental health diagnoses shared their truth—some of them for the first time. They talked about what it's like to be labeled, to be misunderstood, and to live in bodies that don't always cooperate. But more importantly, they talked about rising anyway.

This project reminded me of my own physical limitations and how easy it is to let a diagnosis define you. But these authors chose differently. They chose to define themselves by their dreams, not their diagnoses. They chose to find power in their pain and to speak life where others spoke limits. And the community that was birthed out of this project? It was pure magic. They check on each other, pray for each other, and remind each other that no one has to walk this road alone.

Each anthology has taught me something new about collective healing. They've shown me that healing isn't always loud. Sometimes it's in the quiet moments of connection. Sometimes it's in the silent nods that say, "Me too." Sometimes it's in the courage to write your story even when your hands are trembling.

I've watched authors find freedom in the pages they once feared to write. I've witnessed strangers become family. I've seen chains fall, burdens lifted, and joy restored. Not because everything was fixed—but because someone finally felt seen. Someone finally said, "You too? I thought it was just me."

Pa-Pro-Vi Publishing was never just about books. It was about ministry. About mission. About moments of divine connection where healing could take place—one story at a time.

And to anyone reading this: know that your story matters. Whether you're ready to share it now or still working up the courage, trust that your voice has value. Trust that someone is waiting on the other side of your testimony—because when we heal out loud, we give others permission to do the same.

The power of collective healing is real. And I thank God every day that He allowed me to witness it firsthand.

There is undeniable power in a shared testimony. When one person speaks, others are healed. When many speak, generations are transformed. The stories in these anthologies are living proof that God still uses our voices to break chains—not just for ourselves, but for those who come behind us.

Chapter 11
Trusting the Voice Within

"Your word is a lamp to my feet and a light to my path." —Psalm 119:105 (NKJV)

There's a whisper inside of us—steady, quiet, often drowned out by the storm—but always present. It's the voice of the Creator, speaking light into our days, clarity into our confusion, and courage into our doubts.

Learning to hear that voice is the most radical act of faith I've ever practiced. And in the midst of chronic pain and lupus, it became my lifeline.

For years, I looked for answers in medical charts, doctors' diagnoses, prescriptions. I was living with chronic pain so deep it felt like fire beneath my skin. I had Lupus—a name that carried every potential symptom, every scare, every unknown. And most days, I felt like my body was betraying me. But what God taught me in that weakness changed the way I listen forever.

Because the louder my body screamed, the quieter His voice had to become for me to hear.

Trusting God's voice isn't flashy. It doesn't come with fireworks. It comes in the stillness between pain and prayer. In the pause between medicine and surrender. In the moment I decided not to text someone for validation, but to open my Bible for affirmation.

For me, it started one morning in my living room. I had been up most of the night with pain—my joints screaming as if they forgot their purpose. Tears had stained the pillow. Prayers had been half-formed. I felt alone. I felt small. I felt like maybe God called me to relief, not to rise in pain.

I stumbled to my chair and opened my Bible. My fingers landed on Psalm 46:10: *"Be still, and know that I am God."* In that moment, God wasn't calling me to healing that day. He was calling me to trust the healer.

That whispered truth was more powerful than any counselor's words, any article I'd ever read, or any prescription I'd ever been given.

I had to retrain my heart.

My years of being told that my worth came from productivity, accolades, validation from others—all of it needed recalibration. I used to look at other people's feedback as my compass. But that compass can fail. People's opinions shift. Flaws get exposed. Praise can fade.

God's voice? Never.

Over time, I learned to distinguish between three voices:

- **The voice of fear**: "You'll never be well. You're not strong enough. You don't deserve this healing."

- **The voice of the crowd**: "People expect you to be perfect. People expect you to do more. You will let them down."

- **The Voice within**: *"My grace is sufficient for you—I am enough in your weakness."*

It wasn't easy to quiet the first two, but with every step of faith, the divine Voice grew clearer.

When I started Pa-Pro-Vi Publishing, people questioned me. "You're sick. You limp. How will you help others?" My reply was simple: *Because I've been there.*

I had to trust God's call, not their doubts. I had to say yes even when no one else could see it. And with each author I helped into their story, I learned to trust His voice more.

There were late nights when I had migraine-like pain, yet I coached a woman through her first pages. There were mornings I couldn't dress myself, and I still prayed over a manuscript. And every time, God reminded me that divine guidance doesn't require perfect health—it just requires trusting obedience.

Discernment isn't about choosing between two physical paths. It's about choosing between voices. It's walking forward in peace when fear tried to detain you. It's leaning on God's promises when circumstances scream the opposite.

When Lupus flared hard, and anxiety threatened to drown me. I lay in my bed, body aching, mind spinning with "what ifs."

And God whispered: *"I know your condition—every cell. I am with you. Even here."*

That whisper was the armor that carried me through the night. Not healing the body instantly—but strengthening the spirit.

Trusting that voice changed how I parented, how I ministered, how I built. It became the foundation of every decision.

When opportunities came that seemed beyond my capacity, I learned to consult deeper than my doubts. When physical limitations tried to shrink my dreams, I learned to listen louder to the Voice within.

One of the toughest lessons? Learning to say no.

The world measures success by output. "How many books?" "How many authors?" "How many events?" And in seasons of pain, I had to relearn, "God's validation counts even when no one applauds." That meant declining speaking requests, slowing down on new clients, even pausing publishing deadlines. And in the quiet, I still heard approval—from Him.

Because divine guidance doesn't minimize vision—it recalibrates it.

Through this journey, I've also learned the healing power of multiple confirmations.

God will not contradict Himself. So if you hear guidance in prayer, in Scripture, in peace, and in a trusted voice—lean in. I've seen doors open, closed, redirect—and through each one, I learned to stay aligned with the Voice within.

There was a time I asked God for direction: "What next?"

I prayed and waited. There was nothing. Anxiety surged. I doubted. But I remembered His promise in Jeremiah 29:11—*"I know the plans I have for you… plans to give you hope and a future."*

Months later, I opened my email and an author asked for coaching. I replied. That one yes reignited Pa-Pro-Vi's soul behind the scenes. That one yes came after a period of waiting—quiet, unknown, faithful waiting.

And it reminded me: trusting the voice within isn't always immediate—it's consistent.

I also learned that God's voice isn't always affirming my plans—it sometimes redirects them. He doesn't always lead me up to the mountain. Sometimes He leads me through the valley. Sometimes He changes my prescription.

That's okay.

Discerning His voice meant embracing both: healing and humble surrender. Advancement and holy pause. Victory and divine rest.

When criticism came—about my health, my limitations, or my leadership—I responded with prayer, not defensiveness. I allowed God's voice to be my shield. I didn't need to silence every doubter. I needed to confirm whose calling I walked in.

I often say: *If God speaks it, I do it—even if I'm scared.*

That's the culmination of trusting the voice within: leaning not on my own understanding, but acknowledging Him in all my ways.

Several months ago, I spent a month in a flare—not able to stand without pain. I could've given in to fear. Instead, I spent daily time in Scripture, journaling—leaning into the still small voice. I realized that leadership isn't defined by doing—it's defined by listening and responding. Even in pain.

When I emerged, vision felt sharper. Mercy became deeper. Clarity replaced confusion.

That season taught me: discernment isn't the absence of struggle. It's the presence of God in every season—painful or peaceful.

Let every step forward be lit by His voice—not the clamor of the world, but the certainty of divine direction.

Chapter 12
Permission Denied—Purpose Approved

"But the Lord stood at my side and gave me strength, so that through me the message might be fully proclaimed…"
—2 Timothy 4:17 (NKJV)

There was a time when I believed that being called by God meant being welcomed by people. That if I had a good heart, worked hard, and honored others, they'd invite me in, give me a seat, open doors, or at least hold one open.

That belief was broken.

And what replaced it was something far stronger: **the understanding that God's purpose doesn't require anyone's permission**.

When I first started Pa-Pro-Vi Publishing, I was excited, nervous, and full of vision. I wanted to help people heal through storytelling. I wanted to give voice to the unheard. I wanted to provide what I had needed when I was struggling to share my story—support, clarity, and someone who genuinely cared.

But not everyone shared that vision.

Some people saw me as competition. Others discounted me because I wasn't using their methods. There were people who flat-out told me, "You can't be a part of what we're doing because we're competitors." As if the healing business has room for rivalry.

And then there were the whispers:
"You'll be looking for a real job in six months."
"This is a nice hobby, but it's not sustainable."
"You should follow my formula if you want to succeed."

The truth is, I spent far too much time and energy wanting to be invited to other people's tables. I watched others network, collaborate, support each other, while I waited—hoping someone would extend an invitation. Instead, I got overlooked. Left out. Ignored.

Each "no" pierced a little deeper. Each rejection made me question if I'd misunderstood the assignment.

But it turns out I hadn't misunderstood at all.

God hadn't called me to be *at* their table. He'd called me to *build* mine.

Looking back, I'm thankful for the doors that stayed closed. They forced me to lean fully on God's voice instead of begging for validation from people who couldn't see what He had placed inside me.

I stopped trying to conform.
I stopped trying to be palatable.
I stopped trying to make my purpose "fit" in rooms that weren't built for me.

And I started walking boldly in the purpose God had approved long before I ever heard a single "no."

Was it painful? Absolutely.

Some of the deepest wounds didn't come from strangers—they came from people I trusted. People I supported. People I prayed for. People I cheered on. And yet when it was my turn, they withheld what I had freely given.

Still, I didn't let bitterness grow.
I let *boundaries* grow.
I let *vision* grow.
I let *faith* grow.

The Word says, *"Trust in the Lord with all your heart and lean not on your own understanding."* (Proverbs 3:5)

I had to stop leaning on what I understood and start listening more carefully to God's voice.

His voice said:
Keep going.
Keep building.
Keep believing.
Even when you're not invited. Even when you're not affirmed. Even when you're misunderstood.

Especially then.

Over time, I noticed something beautiful.

The very people who once questioned my ability began to seek my guidance. The same industry that said I wouldn't last began to watch the impact of my work. God was exalting what man had dismissed—not out of spite, but out of purpose.

And I? I just kept showing up.

Helping people tell their stories.
Praying for my clients.

Encouraging people through their pain.
Turning thoughts into realizations.

I realized that **obedience is more powerful than applause**. I learned that *fruitfulness* matters more than fame. I discovered that God's table is big enough for everyone—but when others close the door on you, sometimes He gives you wood, nails, and a hammer instead.

So I started creating space for others who felt like I once did—left out, unheard, unseen.

I invited them to my table.
And together, we told our stories.
And in the telling, we healed.

It wasn't about proving anything anymore. It was about walking in the freedom of knowing I was doing exactly what God called me to do.

I stopped needing permission.

Permission denied? Let them say it.
Purpose approved? Walk in it anyway.

Because I had already been **approved by the One who matters most**.

Because if God gave you the vision, He will also give you the provision, the platform, and the power to fulfill it—**with or without applause.**

Chapter 13
When Your Walk Makes Others Uncomfortable

For do I now persuade men, or God? Or do I seek to please men? For if I still pleased men, I would not be a bondservant of Christ.
—Galatians 1:10 (NKJV)

There's something unexplainably powerful about walking boldly in your calling—especially when you know that calling came straight from God. But there's also something uncomfortable about it—especially for those around you. Not because you're doing anything wrong, but because your obedience exposes their complacency. Your light shines in places they were content to keep dark. Your courage challenges their comfort.

And if you're not careful, you'll start shrinking to make other people feel safe in your presence.

But I made a decision: I will no longer apologize for being who God called me to be. I'm not toning down the light. I'm not watering down the message. I'm not asking for permission to live on purpose.

As I look back, I can confidently say—I am *grateful*. The good. The bad. The uncomfortable. The victorious. All of it.

Because through every experience—whether celebrated or criticized—I found deeper clarity about who I am and, more importantly, *whose* I am.

There were many high moments, moments that made me smile from the inside out. Projects were completed. Authors were launched. Lives were changed. But there were also painful, confusing moments—moments of betrayal, moments of rejection, moments of silence that felt louder than words.

And still, *God was there through it all.*

People can debate all day whether or not God is real. But for me, there is no question. His presence is not just something I read about in Scripture—it's something I've lived through in my own body, in my own home, in my own mind. Every moment confirmed what I already knew: I am never alone.

Some years brought me hard lessons, difficult lessons, and beautiful lessons. The kind that don't just teach you *what* to do differently—they teach you *who* you truly are.

One of those lessons was about awareness—spiritual, emotional, relational, and personal awareness.

As someone who works with people from all walks of life—different backgrounds, cultures, personalities, faiths, and belief systems—awareness is not optional for me. It's essential. Being aware of who *I* am is foundational to how I love people, how I serve them, and how I do business with them.

Awareness is the lens through which I see clearly what I will and will not tolerate. It helps me hear what's being said *and* what's being left unsaid. It's how I discern what aligns with my values and what I need to lovingly walk away from.

I found myself in more than a few situations where others tried to impose their expectations on me—pressuring me to respond a certain way, believe a certain thing, or agree with something that didn't sit well in my spirit.

And in those moments, the loudest voice wasn't theirs.

It was God's.

And His voice reminded me: *Stay true to who I made you to be.*

One person told me I was "too emotional"—as if my ability to empathize was a weakness. That comment stuck with me longer than I'd like to admit. I sat with it, wrestled with it, and then finally... I released it.

Because here's what I know: **God gave me a tender heart on purpose**.

I *am* emotional. And I *should* be. My calling is wrapped in compassion. My purpose is soaked in empathy. My ministry is built on connection—and that requires a heart that feels deeply.

So no, I am *not* too emotional. I am *perfectly equipped*.

Walking in obedience means I treat people not based on how they treat me, but based on how God instructs me to love them. It means I operate from grace, even when I'm disrespected. I speak truth in love, even when others speak lies in pride. I respond with kindness, even when I'm met with cruelty.

My good friend often says, "There's nothing wrong in you that a change in me can't fix." That one sentence has helped me reframe so many interactions—reminding me that I don't have to *match* someone's energy. I just have to reflect *God's* character.

Now, let's be honest: not everyone appreciates that.

There are people who've tried to silence my voice. Dim my light. Redirect my purpose. People who were uncomfortable simply because I didn't fold under pressure, follow their blueprint, or ask for their approval.

But here's the truth: **when you walk in obedience, it will make others uncomfortable**—not because of what you're doing wrong, but because of what you're doing right.

That's why knowing who you are—and whose you are—is so important.

Self-awareness is not just a personal development concept. It's a spiritual discipline. It's the ability to recognize your thoughts, emotions, and values and understand how they influence your behavior and your relationships.

According to Social and Emotional Learning (SEL), self-awareness is defined as the ability to accurately recognize one's emotions and thoughts and understand their influence on behavior. But for me, it goes even deeper.

It's knowing that I am both *flawed* and *favored*. It's understanding that while I am human, I am also holy—set apart, not by perfection, but by purpose.

Luke 11:35 says:

"Therefore take heed that the light which is in you is not darkness."

That scripture reminds me to check my motives, check my attitude, and stay connected to the true Source of my light. Because sometimes, even well-meaning people can mislabel your light as pride or arrogance—when really, it's just obedience.

I've learned to remain rooted in the truth of God's Word. Because if I allow the criticisms of others to define me, I'll begin to doubt the very thing God affirmed in me.

There were seasons when people's discomfort with my walk led to distance. Invitations stopped. Phone calls slowed down. People I once supported no longer supported me. Some said I changed. Others just disappeared without explanation.

It hurt. Deeply.

But it also clarified what was real.

Because the people who can't handle your purpose were never assigned to your journey in the first place.

I've been talked about. Mocked. Misunderstood. But I've also been *kept*.

By God's grace, I've built spaces where others who've been overlooked, dismissed, or rejected can finally feel seen, heard, and valued.

It didn't happen because I was always accepted. It happened because I was obedient—even when I was rejected.

So, if your walk is making others uncomfortable— keep walking.

Don't shrink. Don't silence yourself. Don't compromise your calling.

Because the same God who *called* you will *cover* you. And the same light that makes some people squint is the same light that will help someone else find their way.

Walk on, purposefully and unapologetically.

Chapter 14
The Weight of Being Chosen

"You did not choose Me, but I chose you and appointed you that you should go and bear fruit, and that your fruit should remain, that whatever you ask the Father in My name He may give you."
-John 15:16 (NKJV)

Being chosen by God is both a divine privilege and a humbling responsibility.

It sounds like an honor—and it is. But it also comes with a weight that can't always be explained. It's the kind of weight that settles in your spirit, not just your shoulders. It changes the way you walk, the way you see people, the way you carry yourself in rooms that you once entered casually. The moment you recognize the calling on your life, the weight of obedience begins to reshape everything around you—and within you.

It took me years to understand what that weight truly meant. I used to think being chosen was about status, about being favored, about doors opening with ease. But now, I know that being chosen doesn't always come with applause. Sometimes, it comes with isolation. Sometimes, it comes with tears. And most times, it comes with a responsibility that most people will never see or understand.

But it also comes with grace. And that grace is what keeps me going.

To be a **woman of resilience** in a world filled with chaos means embodying strength, grace, and determination in the face of adversity. It's about navigating uncertainty with courage, standing firm in your purpose, and emerging stronger despite life's storms. It's about saying "yes" to God—even when you don't have all the answers, even when people walk away, even when the pain of the journey feels unbearable.

That's the weight of being chosen.

1. Choosing Strength Over Surrender

Resilience isn't about pretending everything is okay. It's not about masking your tears behind a smile or forcing yourself to keep pushing when your soul is exhausted. No, resilience is about acknowledging the pain and moving forward anyway. It's about saying, "This hurts," and still choosing to show up.

There have been so many moments in my journey where I felt like giving up. Times when my body was in too much pain to move. Times when my heart was too heavy to speak. Times when I prayed and heard silence. But even in those moments, something in me refused to quit. Maybe it was stubbornness. Maybe it was desperation. But now I know—it was *God's strength* showing up in my weakness.

A resilient woman may bend, but she won't break.

2. Standing on Faith

When you're chosen, you don't get to walk by sight. You walk by faith. And let me tell you—faith isn't always glamorous. Sometimes, faith looks like crying yourself to sleep and waking up to do the very thing God called you to do anyway. Sometimes it's trusting a promise that hasn't shown up yet. Sometimes, it's believing God will make a way while staring at a mountain you don't know how to climb.

In a chaotic world, faith becomes your lifeline. When the world feels like it's spinning out of control, faith steadies your steps. It reminds you that *God is still in control—even when nothing around you looks like it.* There have been moments in my life—especially while living with chronic pain and navigating lupus—when all I had was faith. No roadmap. No backup plan. Just God's voice telling me to keep going.

And I did.

3. Adapting to Change

There's one thing life will always guarantee: *change*. It doesn't ask for permission. It doesn't wait for your readiness. It just shows up—sometimes gently, sometimes forcefully—but always with a purpose.

Being a resilient woman means learning to adapt without losing your identity. It means embracing change without compromising your values. I've had to shift in ways I never anticipated—personally, professionally, and spiritually. I had to adjust to life as an empty nester, where my children are now adults, making their own choices, living their own lives. That shift was both liberating and unsettling.

But even as everything around me changed, I remained grounded in who I am in God. And that foundation kept me from losing myself in the process.

4. Leading with Purpose

I didn't set out to be a leader. I didn't wake up one day and say, "I want to inspire people." I was just trying to survive. I was just trying to make sense of my story. I was just trying to heal.

But in the process of healing, *God gave me a ministry.*

The stories I've published, the authors I've coached, the women I've mentored—all of that is part of a greater purpose I never saw coming. It's not about me—it's about the people I've been assigned to. It's about showing them that you can still lead with integrity, still speak with truth, and still love people deeply, even when life has broken you.

That's what leadership rooted in purpose looks like.

It's not about power. It's about service.

5. Practicing Self-Care

Carrying a divine assignment doesn't mean running yourself into the ground. One of the hardest lessons I've had to learn is that *I can't pour from an empty cup*. Rest is holy. Boundaries are biblical. Stillness is necessary.

I've learned to give myself permission to rest—not just physically, but emotionally and spiritually. I've learned to say no without guilt. I've learned that silence is not weakness—it's wisdom.

Taking care of myself doesn't mean I'm selfish. It means I'm aware of the value of what I carry—and I treat it with care.

6. Embracing Vulnerability

For a long time, I thought strength meant having it all together. I thought people only respected you if you never showed weakness. But I've learned that vulnerability is one of the greatest displays of strength.

I've cried in front of authors. I've broken down during interviews. I've shared parts of my story I never thought I'd say out loud. And you know what? It didn't make people run—it made them feel seen. Because people aren't looking for perfection—they're looking for *realness*.

Being chosen doesn't mean you have to be invincible. It means you trust God enough to be transparent. It means you allow others to see your scars—not for pity, but for permission. Permission for them to heal, to speak, to rise.

The weight of being chosen is heavy. But it is also holy.

God didn't choose me because I was the most qualified. He chose me because I was willing. Willing to say yes. Willing to be stretched. Willing to walk when I didn't know where the path would lead. And in every "yes," I've found healing. In every "yes," I've found purpose. In every "yes," I've seen His glory.

I don't take it lightly. But I don't carry it alone.

Being chosen doesn't mean your life will be easy. But it does mean it will be *purposeful*. And if God called you to it, He will equip you to carry it—with grace, with strength, and with joy.

Don't run from the weight. *Lean into it*. There's glory on the other side.

Chapter 15
Obedience Over Outcome

"Trust in the LORD with all your heart and lean not on your own understanding; in all your ways acknowledge Him And He shall direct your paths."
—Proverbs 3:5-6 (NIV)

When you take God at His word, sometimes it leads you into uncertainty. Sometimes it means stepping out without seeing what's ahead. Obedience doesn't always come with a guarantee of immediate reward. Often, it comes with a promise. Promises aren't always visible. Promises don't have glossy pictures. Promises aren't packaged neatly. But they are real.

And I've learned that when God gives an instruction, your job isn't to fix the outcome—it's to follow the path.

Trusting God in Business

It would have been easier to follow industry paces. To model someone else's roadmap. To build things the "proven" way. But God gave me a different business plan—one rooted in divine guidance, not human formulas.

Every time I launched a series, a book, or a workshop, I wasn't always sure how it would turn out. *Walking Limitations* started while I was at the Mayo Clinic. Pa-Pro-Vi Publishing birthed from a single phone call in a hotel room. I didn't have a financial forecast. I didn't have marketing expertise. I just had God's voice saying, *"It's time."*

Learning to trust God in business meant trusting that He would be faithful—even when the calendar didn't show a packed room, even when the startup funds were low, even when the risk looked greater than the reward.

And time and again, I watched Him show up—in unexpected clients, in divine connections, in feedback that changed lives, including mine.

Trusting God with Family

As my children grew into independent adults, the dynamics shifted. My business needed more of me. My body required more rest. My heart wrestled with letting go. I could have convinced myself I had to choose—business or family.

But obedience told me: *No*. God said, "You can have both."

So I began trusting Him in my family life. I showed up for —even though they didn't need me. I asked about their work, their dreams, their worries. I scheduled calls. I remembered birthdays. I laughed hard. I cried with them when life got hard. And I prayed over them—daily, deeply—without shrinking my business hours, but expanding my faith that God could handle both.

I learned that obedience in business and obedience in motherhood didn't have to compete. They both came from the same place of trust: *God is faithful in every assignment He gives you.*

Trusting God with My Health

Lupus. Chronic pain. Unpredictable flare-ups. Good days. Bad days. There was no pattern. No guarantee. I could follow my treatments perfectly and still face intense pain without warning.

God didn't promise immediate healing. He didn't guarantee a pain-free life. But He promised presence.

So I obeyed—trusting His rhythm over the world's timetable. When the pain flared, I rested. When doctors couldn't help, I worshiped. When frustration rose, I prayed. When fear knocked, I leaned on Scriptures like "My grace is sufficient."

Obedience looked like following medical advice and trusting God's medicine at the same time. Obedience meant listening to my body and obeying my spirit. It looked like advocacy when necessary and surrender at other times.

It meant acknowledging vulnerability—not as weakness, but as opportunity to trust more deeply.

Trusting God in Faith

There were seasons where prayer felt silent. Seasons where Bible study felt heavy. Seasons where I questioned the purpose of blessing in the middle of pain. Those were tests of obedience too.

It would have been easier to walk away. But obedience whispered: *Hold on.*

So I prayed anyway. I opened the Word anyway. I praised anyway. Even when I didn't feel it. Even when everything around me seemed to contradict every promise I had ever claimed.

I learned that faith isn't a feeling. It's a posture. It's a decision. And obedience meant holding steady in that posture—regardless of the uncertainty.

When Obedience Looks Weird

I've had people quietly question my choices.

- Why walk with limitations and still start a publishing company?
- Why invest emotionally in authors with no experience?
- Why keep writing when healing hadn't arrived?
- Why speak up about faith in places where silence was easier?

At times it felt lonely.

But obedience doesn't fit neatly into someone else's comfort zone. Obedience feels radical. It looks different. It demands faith over convenience.

I remember sitting in a boardroom pitch and hearing someone say, "It doesn't make sense." And I realized—

they didn't understand the assignment. I had to choose obedience over their doubt.

Waiting Without Worrying

There were times I obeyed and saw immediate results. There were other times I obeyed and heard nothing for months. But waiting didn't become worrying.

Matthew 25:21 says, *"Well done, good and faithful servant... enter into the joy of your lord."* Success in heaven doesn't depend on human trophy cases. It depends on faithfulness.

Sometimes obedience brings reward quickly. Sometimes it doesn't.

But obedience always honors God.

The Emotional Landscape of Obedience

Obedience can be exhausting.

It can feel unbalanced—when you're pouring out more than you're receiving. When your body aches, your heart strains, your soul doubts.

Carrying God's assignment carries weight.

Sometimes you need to cry. Sometimes you need to rest. Sometimes you need to let someone else carry it for a moment—your spouse, a friend, a counselor.

Resilience doesn't mean running on empty. It means recognizing when to refuel. It means obeying not just the call to serve—but the call to self-care.

God honors both kinds of obedience: *doing* and *resting*.

Seeing the Invisible

One of the hardest lessons? Obedience is often invisible.

You may never know the lives you've touched. The hearts you've impacted. The children you've helped heal. The parent who chose differently because they saw you choose to write truth. You may never see the fruit.

Sometimes all you do is sow, kneel and pray for rain, and walk into the next assignment without looking back.

That's faith. That's obedience. That's trust.

Maybe someone you don't even know will one day say, "Your story saved me." And you'll never know how far your obedience traveled.

Holding the Promise When You Don't Feel It

There have been seasons when God told me to keep going.

So I prayed. I obeyed. Yet the results felt grossly delayed. I wrestled with impatience. I wrestled with guilt. I wrestled with fear.

But the Word reminded me: *"Wait on the Lord; be of good courage...He shall strengthen your heart."* (Psalm 27:14)

Obedience looks forward more than it looks back. It walks into the unknown with peace, not panic. It rests in promises, not in finish lines.

Obedience as Freedom

What people often misunderstand is that obedience doesn't limit you—it liberates you.

When I obey God's path for Pa-Pro-Vi, I'm not chained to a strategy—I'm anchored in purpose.

When I obey God in parenting, I'm not trapped by guilt—I'm rooted in grace.

When I obey God in managing chronic illness, I'm not controlled by fear—I'm sustained by faith.

Obedience isn't restrictive—it's empowering.

At the end of the day, obedience isn't about results. It's about relationship. It's about trust. It's about honoring God more than you honor your own understanding.

You will be tested. You will be misunderstood. You will wonder if it's worth it. But let me tell you this:

If God told you to do it, your obedience is already fruitful—even if you don't get to see it now.

Obedience doesn't promise easy outcomes. It promises divine alignment.

When you choose obedience over outcome, you step into a life of purpose—even when the path doesn't make sense. Because God sees the beginning, the middle, and the end.

Walk on.

Obey anyway.

Your faithfulness is your legacy.

Chapter 16
Raising Voices, Not Just Books

"Let the redeemed of the Lord say so, Whom He has redeemed from the hand of the enemy."
—Psalm 107:2 (NIV)

At Pa-Pro-Vi Publishing, storytelling is not just about writing a book—it's a calling. It's ministry. It's healing. It's obedience.

When I launched Pa-Pro-Vi during one of the most difficult seasons of my life, I had no idea I was birthing more than a publishing company—I was birthing purpose. I was still limping, physically and emotionally, when I started helping others write through their pain. What I thought was a temporary project to help someone else became the foundation of my own healing. God was doing something far greater than formatting books and building covers—He was raising voices. He was raising mine.

Today, as the CEO and Founder of Pa-Pro-Vi Publishing, I stand in awe of the stories God entrusts me to help bring forth. We don't just help people publish—we walk with them through transformation. Each manuscript is a testimony in progress. Each chapter a sacred offering. Each story a ministry.

This is how we raise voices...

1. We Create a Safe Space for Authenticity

I've learned that the first step to healing is honesty. Many of the authors I work with have never shared their stories out loud. They come to me timid, uncertain, ashamed, or scared. They whisper secrets into the phone, unsure if their truth deserves to be told.

At Pa-Pro-Vi, I let them know that their story is sacred. That their voice matters. I've sat in sessions where tears flowed before words did. And I never rush that process—because I understand it.

When I wrote *Walking Limitations by Other People's Definition*, I told truths I had kept hidden for decades. I didn't do it for validation—I did it for release. That's what I now offer to others: the courage to say, "This happened... and I'm still standing."

We give authors permission to be raw, to cry, to pause, to be unsure. Because real healing doesn't come in polished lines—it comes in broken honesty.

2. We Celebrate Growth, Not Just Grammar

A story that ends in pain is incomplete. At Pa-Pro-Vi, we encourage our authors to go beyond the trauma. Yes, we tell the truth—but we also highlight the transformation.

Some authors say, "But I'm still in the middle of it." That's okay. So am I. Healing isn't a destination—it's a process. But even in the middle, there's movement. A boundary you set. A prayer you prayed. A day you got out of bed when it felt impossible. Those are victories.

We teach authors how to identify the moments where resilience peeked through the rubble. That's where readers find hope—not in the perfection, but in the progress.

3. We Walk With Our Authors Every Step

No one is just handed a book deal and told, "Good luck." At Pa-Pro-Vi, our authors get mentorship. They get prayer. They get guidance. And they get me.

I walk through their projects with them—whether it's coaching them through timelines, helping them structure chapters, or simply being a sounding board when self-doubt creeps in. I've cried with authors. I've prayed over manuscripts. I've fought for stories that others tried to silence.

This is personal. Every project carries part of my heart because I know what it's like to birth something beautiful while still bleeding.

4. We Help People See Purpose in Their Pain

So many people come to me with stories drenched in shame. Abuse, addiction, abandonment, betrayal... they carry it like a heavy weight, unsure how to lay it down.

But when we start framing their experience through the lens of purpose, something shifts. We ask: *Who might be helped by this story? Who needs to know they're not alone?*

That reframes everything.

Suddenly, the shame becomes testimony. The pain becomes a platform. They realize their story was never just for them. Someone's healing is waiting on their obedience.

5. We Publish Triumph

Every Pa-Pro-Vi book is a celebration. We don't just print stories—we honor them.

From solo books to anthologies, we highlight the resilience behind each story. Whether it's a mother writing about her child's diagnosis, a man sharing how he reclaimed his life after prison, or a woman revealing how she overcame domestic violence—every launch feels like a homecoming.

They didn't just survive. They spoke.

And when they hold their book in their hands, something powerful happens: they remember that they are not just authors. They are victors.

6. We Build Community, Not Just Catalogs

Healing happens in connection. That's why we cultivate community among our authors.

Through anthology groups, coaching sessions, and private support chats, our authors uplift each other.

They exchange encouragement, feedback, and sometimes even lifelong friendships.

In this community, no one walks alone. No one's voice goes unheard. We carry each other's burdens—and that makes the healing even sweeter.

Transformation in Action: Raising Voices Through Anthologies

I've seen firsthand how group storytelling multiplies healing:

- **I Did It: Teen Mom Success** broke stereotypes and stigma. Twelve women turned shame into strategy, showing young moms that success is still possible—even with early detours.

- **Our Journey From Girls to Women** spotlighted the sacred transformation of womanhood—through abuse, confusion, faith, and freedom.

- **Our Journey From Boys to Men** gave men the rare space to speak truth without judgment. They reflected on masculinity, fatherhood, fear, and faith in powerful ways.

- **The Women of the Waiting Room** captured the hard pause between promise and manifestation—reminding us that God is still present even in our delays.

- **She Said Yes To Herself Unapologetically** helped women break free from people-pleasing and say "yes" to purpose, worth, and healing.

- **Addicted to Bliss** shined light on hidden struggles—from emotional eating to perfectionism—showing how we can turn harmful habits into holy healing.

- **We Choose to Be More Than Our Diagnoses** amplified the voices of those living with chronic illness and mental health challenges, proving that limitations do not define purpose.

Every anthology raised more than words—it raised *voices*. And in doing so, it birthed healing in both authors and readers.

Why It Matters in the Kingdom

At Pa-Pro-Vi, we don't just help people tell stories. We help them reclaim identity. We help them see their worth. We help them walk in purpose—not permission.

God doesn't need your resume—He needs your "yes." He doesn't wait for you to feel ready—He equips you as you go.

I know this because I've lived it. There were days I didn't feel qualified to lead a publishing house. Days when the pain in my body made it hard to get out of bed. Days when I was told my work didn't matter.

But I kept going. Not because I had all the answers, but because I had *obedience*. I knew my "yes" wasn't just about me—it was for someone else's breakthrough.

Raising voices is my purpose. It's not just a business. It's a divine assignment.

Raising voices is holy work. It's not always glamorous. It's often uncomfortable. But it's worth it.

Because every time someone finds the courage to speak, heaven leans in and listens.

That's the ministry of storytelling.

That's the mission of Pa-Pro-Vi.

That's the *purpose* I walk in—by God's design.

Chapter 17
Healing Is a Lifetime Journey

"Then those who feared the Lord spoke to one another, And the Lord listened and heard them; So a book of remembrance was written before Him For those who fear the Lord And who meditate on His name." —Malachi 3:16 (NKJV)

Healing. It's a word often spoken with finality, as if it's a destination to arrive at and check off like an item on a to-do list. But what I've come to know deeply—through pain, progress, and the relentless grace of God—is that healing is not a finish line.

It's a daily choice. A breath-by-breath journey.

It's in the way we speak to ourselves in the mirror. In the courage it takes to get out of bed on days when the weight of memory sits heavy.

It's in how we learn to forgive others—sometimes again and again—and especially, how we learn to forgive ourselves.

Healing is layered. It's messy. It's sacred.

And most importantly, it's *ours*.

There was a time in my life when I thought healing meant perfection—when I equated wholeness with the absence of pain. I believed if I could just *get through* the next hardship, I'd finally be free. But pain taught me what comfort couldn't. God taught me, in His divine wisdom, that healing wasn't about being pain-free. It was about being fear-free. Shame-free. Free to be who He designed me to be.

And part of that freedom came from discovering the power in my own story—and encouraging others to do the same.

Becoming Authentic

Share your story. Be true to yourself. Be you. Be authentic.

These phrases sound beautiful, but for a long time, they felt like foreign concepts to me. How could I be authentic when I didn't even fully know who I was? For so long, I lived to please. I smiled when I wanted to cry. I agreed to things that didn't sit right with my spirit. I avoided conflict. I sought approval like it was oxygen.

I wanted to make people happy. I didn't want anyone to be upset with me. So I adapted. I adjusted. I performed.

And somewhere in the process, I forgot what my own voice sounded like.

But as I grew older—and God peeled back the layers—I began to see my reflection more clearly. I began to accept my limitations. To recognize that I was different, and that difference wasn't a defect. It was design.

I realized I didn't want to be like anyone else.

That realization didn't happen overnight, but when it did, it gave birth to something extraordinary.

Pa-Pro-Vi Publishing was born not just as a company, but as a calling. And it wasn't created in a season of perfection. It came in a season of pain—a divine disruption. I was still healing. I *am* still healing. But I had learned enough about my own journey to help others see the value in theirs.

The Call to Purpose

When I first launched Pa-Pro-Vi, the support I received from my inner circle was overwhelmingly positive. But there were also subtle (and not-so-subtle) doubts.

"Don't you think you're doing too much?"
"What about your health?"
"Shouldn't you wait until things settle down?"

And there was the one that still echoes sometimes: "You'll be looking for a real job in six months."

Those words stung. Not because I needed approval—but because I had just started learning how to trust myself, and the enemy knows how to strike when your confidence is still fragile.

But I didn't let their doubts become my truth.

Instead, I held tight to the only voice that mattered—God's. And I clung to the belief that there was purpose in what I was building, even if no one else could see it yet.

Honoring the Process

Healing and authenticity go hand in hand. But walking authentically comes with a price. It means being willing to be misunderstood. It means choosing vulnerability over validation. It means giving up the comfort of blending in for the courage to stand out.

The world tells us to be agreeable, to follow trends, to keep quiet if our truth is uncomfortable. But authenticity requires us to challenge that. It demands honesty—even when it's messy. Especially when it's messy.

I read an article once in *Scientific American* that said people feel most authentic when they conform to certain socially accepted traits—being agreeable, emotionally stable, intellectual. And while I respect the research, I've lived the truth: I feel most authentic when I'm honest.

When I'm real.

When I cry and laugh in the same breath.
When I talk about my pain without wrapping it in a bow.

When I walk into a room not trying to impress—but trying to *connect*.

That's what authenticity has come to mean to me. And that's what I try to offer through every author I work with.

A Passion for People

Even before I found my authentic self, I've always had a passion for people. A desire to understand them. To get to the "why" behind the behavior. To find the little child hiding behind adult wounds.

What happened to them?
What shaped their view of themselves?
Who told them they weren't enough?

These questions fueled me as I stepped into the work of helping others tell their stories. I didn't want to duplicate what anyone else was doing. I wanted to *listen* first. To see the person behind the pages. To help them find the words they didn't know they needed.

And in helping them speak—I found my own voice.

Healing Through Storytelling

At Pa-Pro-Vi Publishing, we've never been just about books. We're about healing. We're about courage. We're about creating a sacred space for stories that often go untold.

Every time an author shares their truth, they move closer to wholeness. And every time I help them do that, so do I.

The stories I've witnessed—the raw, gut-wrenching, redemptive, faith-filled testimonies—have changed me. They've reminded me that pain is not the end of the story. That victory isn't just possible—it's promised.

And they've affirmed, time and time again, that healing is a lifetime journey.

The Grace to Become

One of the greatest lessons I've learned is this:

You are not behind—you are becoming.

Healing doesn't happen on a schedule. It isn't linear. Some days, you feel strong. Other days, you feel like you're starting over. But both days are holy. Both days count.

I've had to show myself grace when my body betrayed me. I've had to show myself patience when my emotions overwhelmed me. I've had to learn how to *honor my pace*—especially as a mother of adult children and a grandmother.

My role has shifted. My house is quieter. My needs have changed. But my mission hasn't.

I still show up every day with the intention to pour, to encourage, to speak life—not just into others, but into myself.

And that too... is healing.

Reflections of Grace

Sometimes I look back on the girl I used to be—the one who tried so hard to fit in, to be liked, to be chosen—and I grieve for her. But I also celebrate her. Because she survived. She fought. She kept going long enough for me to become this version of myself.

The healed one.
The healing one.

The one who shows up in truth, even if her voice shakes.

And in that, I've discovered that healing isn't a destination.

It's a daily "yes."
A quiet surrender.
A whispered prayer.
A deep breath.
A sacred pause.
A walk by faith, not by sight.

Your healing is not behind.
Your process is not wrong.
You are not too late.
You are becoming—day by day, step by step, by God's design.

So take the next breath.
Write the next page.
Speak the next truth.
And walk forward in grace.

Because healing isn't a past-tense event.
It's a present-tense journey.
And you, dear heart, are still becoming.

Chapter 18

Resting Without Guilt

"Come to Me, all you who labor and are heavy laden, and I will give you rest. Take My yoke upon you and learn from Me, for I am gentle and lowly in heart, and you will find rest for your souls. For My yoke is easy and My burden is light."
— *Matthew 11:28-30 (NKJV)*

For as long as I can remember, I have been a woman who keeps moving.

Moving through the pain.
Moving through the pressure.
Moving through the noise, the expectations, the appointments, the responsibilities.
Pushing through—because that's what strong women do, right?

We push.
We press.
We persevere.

And somewhere in that rhythm of strength, I forgot how to rest.

Not just sleep. Not just closing my eyes for a few hours between deadlines. I mean real rest—the kind that lets your soul take a deep breath. The kind that allows you to *pause* without shame. The kind that says, "This moment is holy too."

I have always been a doer. Even in pain, even in grief, even in chaos—I kept going. Not because I wanted to be a martyr or prove something, but because movement made me feel useful. It helped distract me from discomfort. It helped me feel worthy.

But pushing through everything—even God's invitation to rest—will eventually leave you empty.

There came a point when my body started speaking louder than my to-do list. It whispered at first. Then it yelled. Then it shut down. And I realized: I had confused busyness with purpose. I had confused exhaustion with obedience.

I had equated rest with weakness.

The Divine Invitation to Stop

God, in His loving patience, started teaching me that rest isn't a reward—it's a requirement. He's not waiting at the finish line of my productivity with a crown. He's walking with me through every moment saying, "Daughter, stop. Breathe. Be."

I began to learn how to rest—not because I was finished—but because I was *faithful*.

Faithful enough to trust that the world wouldn't fall apart if I paused.
Faithful enough to believe that I was still valuable, even when I wasn't producing.
Faithful enough to remember that even God rested— *not because He was tired, but because He was done.*

Listening to My Body

For years, I ignored my body. I told it to wait. I told it to keep up. I told it to push through. And my body obeyed—until it couldn't anymore.

Living with chronic pain and lupus has been one of my greatest teachers. Not just because it humbles me, but because it *slows me*. It teaches me that rest is not the opposite of strength—it is part of it.

I am learning to listen to the whispers:

"You're tired. Stop now."
"You've done enough today. Breathe."

"This moment doesn't need your effort—it needs your presence."

Rest is now part of my rhythm. Not always perfectly. Not without resistance. But more intentionally than ever before.

Smelling the Roses

My favorite uncle tells me all the time: "Work is good, but rest is better." And I'm finally starting to understand what he means.

There's something holy in simply *being*.

In watching the sunset without checking your phone.
In letting yourself laugh without thinking about what's next.
In choosing a nap over a meeting.
In turning the ringer off and turning the gratitude up.

Sometimes I stop in the middle of a busy day and go outside just to feel the air. I take a walk. I listen to the birds. I sit on the porch and smell the roses—literally. I remind myself that this world is not mine to carry. It belongs to God. And He's already holding it all together.

What a freeing truth: I don't have to run to be seen. I don't have to hustle to be heard. I don't have to over-function to be loved.

I just have to *be*.

Letting Go of Guilt

One of the hardest things about learning to rest has been letting go of the guilt.

When I first began canceling appointments or saying "no" to engagements because my body needed stillness, I felt selfish. Lazy. Irresponsible.

But that was the lie.

The truth? Rest is not a sin.
Rest is not indulgent.
Rest is not procrastination.

Rest is obedience.

God commands rest—He modeled it in Genesis and invited us into it in Exodus. Jesus withdrew from the crowds. He went away to pray. He napped in the middle of storms.

And if Jesus—the Son of God—rested, why do I think I have to keep proving myself by running until I collapse?

It's not faith to keep going when God tells you to stop.

It's fear.

So I'm choosing to honor rest. Not as a luxury—but as an act of spiritual alignment.

Rest as Worship

What I've discovered is that resting isn't just physical—it's emotional, mental, and spiritual too.

It's releasing outcomes and trusting God with the "in-between."
It's stepping away from the noise and letting His Word fill the silence.
It's journaling your prayers, crying without shame, or simply doing nothing—and knowing that's enough.

Some of my sweetest moments with God have come not in the busy hours of doing, but in the still moments of being.

I've stopped measuring my worth by my output. I've stopped tying my identity to how many people I help or how much I accomplish. I've started asking different questions:

"Am I at peace today?"
"Did I show up with love today?"
"Did I honor my body today?"
"Did I listen for God's whisper today?"

And if I can answer "yes" to any of those... it's been a productive day.

The Journey Continues

I'm still learning this. I still struggle sometimes. I still get caught in the rhythm of overdoing. I still have moments when guilt tries to creep in—when I worry about how others will perceive my rest, or when I feel like I've let someone down by not showing up.

But I've come too far to go back.

I've seen what happens when I rest:
My creativity returns.
My compassion deepens.
My clarity sharpens.
My spirit softens.
And my relationship with God deepens.

Rest brings me back to myself. To Him. To the purpose He designed me for.

A Final Thought

If you're tired, stop.

If you're overwhelmed, pause.

If you're carrying more than you were meant to, lay it down.

You don't have to keep proving. You don't have to keep pushing. You don't have to exhaust yourself to be worthy of rest.

You are already enough.

And the One who called you will not love you less for honoring the boundaries of your humanity.

He made you with limits. He knew you'd need naps. He knew your shoulders weren't built to carry the whole world.

So let go. Lay down the guilt. Embrace the pause.

And rest—not just as relief—but as worship.

Chapter 19
My Walk, My Worship

"I beseech you therefore, brethren, by the mercies of God, that you present your bodies a living sacrifice, holy, acceptable to God, which is your reasonable service." —Romans 12:1 (NIV)

My walk is not just a physical motion—it is a posture of worship. Every limp. Every scar. Every tear I've cried in the quiet moments. Every step that hurt but I took anyway. They are all offerings—laid on the altar of obedience, covered in grace, soaked in faith.

There are those who would look at a life marked by limitations and see only weakness. But I've come to see it differently. I've come to understand that what the world calls limitation, God can use as invitation— an invitation to draw closer to Him, to lean not on my own understanding, but to rest in the knowledge that He walks with me, limp and all.

When I was a little girl and a medical mistake left me with a lifetime of walking limitations, I didn't know what worship really meant. I didn't know that decades later, those very limitations would become a lifeline between me and the Father. I didn't know that the pain in my body would teach me how to listen for the whisper of God's voice, how to depend on His strength, how to offer up not perfection, but presence.

I've heard people say, "Why would a good God let something like that happen to you?"
But here's the truth: I never blamed God. Not once. Not when I had to learn how to walk again. Not when the pain showed up in my bones like an uninvited guest. Not even when I felt invisible in rooms full of people who didn't understand.

If anything, my limitations brought me to His feet. And staying there taught me how to truly live.

I don't worship God because I'm whole. I worship Him because I'm His.
I don't serve Him because I'm perfect. I serve Him because He perfects me through His love.
And my walk—this beautiful, imperfect, halting walk— is my offering back to Him.

Worship in Spirit and Truth

One of the greatest blessings in my life has been teaching Bible study. It's not about standing at a podium or quoting every verse with flawless recall. It's about bringing your heart, your story, and your truth to the table. It's about letting God speak through your broken places.

When I teach, I don't hide behind the scriptures—I bring them into my life. I weave them into my story. I tell the truth about what it means to hurt and still believe. I speak from a place of faith that has been tested, not imagined.

Worshipping God in spirit and truth is not about me, it's about Him. It's about rising from bed when the pain is great and I don't feel like getting up. It's fellowship with my brothers and sisters in Christ. It's serving someone even while in pain. It's pausing in the middle of a storm and saying, "Thank You!"

My walk—literal and spiritual—is not just movement; it's ministry. It's how I show God that I still trust Him, even when my body tries to tell me otherwise.

Faith Over Frustration

I'll be honest, it's not always easy. Living with chronic pain and navigating life with lupus isn't something you just get used to. It tests you. It drains you. And it challenges you to decide whether you're going to stay bitter or grow better.

But the grace of God has been my anchor.

There are days when I want to be frustrated. Days when I want to give up. But I remind myself that every time I get up and walk—no matter how slow, no matter how painful—it's a declaration: *God, I still trust You.*

And even when I'm limping, I'm worshiping.

I've come to realize that God is not impressed with our hustle, our image, or our striving. He wants our hearts. He wants our effort. Not our perfection.

My worship isn't polished—it's personal.

I talk to God like a daughter who needs her Daddy. I cry in His presence when the world feels heavy. I laugh with Him when He shows up in unexpected ways. I write down prayers in the pages of my journal.

I play music when I need a reminder that I'm not alone.

He meets me there. Every time.

Walking My Talk

I do my best to live what I teach. I try to walk my talk—not because I want people to see me as flawless, but because I want them to see me as faithful. There's a difference.

Faithfulness doesn't mean I never struggle. It means I keep showing up even when I do.

People often ask me how I manage to do all that I do—with Pa-Pro-Vi, with my family, with my health challenges—and still seem to hold it all together. The truth? I don't. Not all the time.

But God does.

He holds me together. He reminds me that my walk is not just for me—it's for someone watching who needs to know that pain doesn't disqualify them from purpose. That a limp doesn't mean they can't lead. That brokenness doesn't cancel their calling.

This Walk Is for Generations

One of the greatest joys in my life is being a mother and grandmother. As my children have grown and now have children of their own, I'm reminded that my walk is a legacy.

They watch how I navigate struggle. How I pray. How I speak life. How I serve even when I'm tired. They may not remember every lesson I teach, but they'll remember how I lived.

And I want them to know that their walk—whatever it looks like—is worthy of worship too.

I want them to know that obedience sometimes looks like rest. That surrender sometimes looks like taking the next step, even if you're scared. That faith is not always loud—but it's always powerful.

Worship Is My Response

When life gets heavy, I worship.
When my body aches, I worship.
When people don't understand, I worship.
When everything goes right—and when nothing does—I worship.

Because He is still God. And I am still His.

There's something holy about choosing to worship through the weight. It's not denial. It's not pretending everything's okay. It's defiance against despair. It's standing on faith when feelings say otherwise.

This is my walk.
This is my worship.
And even with limitations, I choose to offer it to God—every step, every scar, every breath.

Because walking with Him, even with a limp, is better than running without Him.

Chapter 20
By God's Design

The Lord will perfect that which concerns me; Your mercy, O Lord, endures forever; Do not forsake the work of your hands." —Psalm 138:8 (NKJV)

Looking back over my life—the pain I didn't ask for, the healing I didn't think I deserved, the victories I didn't even see coming—one truth remains clear: it was all *by God's design*.

None of it was random. None of it was wasted. Not the needle that changed my life at four years old. Not the limp I've carried for decades. Not the betrayal, the heartbreak, or the sleepless nights. Not the seasons of silence when I wondered if God still saw me. Not even the detours, the delays, or the closed doors.

It all had purpose.

I didn't always see it. In fact, for a long time I resisted it. I tried to walk in strength that wasn't mine. I tried to carry things God never asked me to carry. I wanted the healing without the process, the purpose without the pain. But God is too wise to waste anything and too loving to let us settle for less than His design.

Everything I thought disqualified me, He used to develop me.

Every "no" I thought was rejection was really redirection.

Every breakdown became groundwork for a breakthrough.

And now I can say with full confidence: *My life may have been touched by limitation, but it is defined by divine intention.*

Living Proof

If you would have told me years ago that my limp would become a platform... that my trauma would birth a publishing company... that my scars would speak louder than my words... I would have smiled politely but doubted quietly.

But here I am.
Still walking.
Still worshiping.
Still healing.

Still writing.

Still helping others tell their stories, because telling mine set me free.

I used to think my story was too broken to be used. I used to wonder if I missed my moment because of everything I had endured. But what I've come to know—deep down in my spirit—is that everything I went through was exactly what I needed to go through. Not because God caused it, but because He allowed it. And when God allows something, He *always* redeems it.

Now I see it clearer than ever: I am living proof that God can use *everything*.

A Life Aligned

There's a peace that comes from walking in alignment. Not perfection. Not performance. But alignment.

To be aligned with God's purpose is to stop striving for validation and start living from identity.

It means I no longer ask for permission to pursue what God has already approved. It means I no longer apologize for taking up space in a world that once made me feel small. It means I don't chase platforms—I build them with God's guidance.

Alignment doesn't mean I have all the answers. It doesn't mean I never feel pain or get discouraged. But it does mean I trust that even when I can't trace God's hand, I can still trust His heart.

I walk in purpose, not permission.

I speak truth, not fear.

I build legacy, not likes.

And I do it all not because I'm qualified by man, but because I'm *chosen* by God.

The True Victory

Victory for me isn't about applause, awards, or accolades. Those things are nice—but they aren't the goal.

Victory is when someone reads *Walking Limitations* and realizes they're not alone.

Victory is when a mother decides to write her story and her child sees her for the first time as more than just "mom," but as a woman of strength.

Victory is when a man who never felt safe enough to cry shares his truth in *Our Journey From Boys to Men* and says, "This set me free."

Victory is when an author who didn't think their voice mattered holds their book in their hands and says, "I did this. I told my truth."

Victory is watching people walk out of shame and into purpose.

That's what I live for. That's what *Pa-Pro-Vi Publishing* was born to do.

Not just to publish books—but to partner with God in setting captives free, one story at a time.

The Weight and the Wonder

Don't get me wrong—this journey hasn't been easy.

There were moments I cried myself to sleep. Moments when the pain in my body screamed louder than the hope in my heart. Times I wanted to quit, cancel everything, and retreat into silence.

But God never let me stay there long.

Because every time I wanted to give up, He reminded me: *This isn't about you. This is about the lives attached to your obedience.*

The weight of being chosen is real. But so is the wonder.

And if you asked me if I'd do it all again—the books, the betrayal, the breakthroughs, the breakdowns—I'd say yes.

Because what God has built in me, through me, and around me is worth it. Every single part.

A Legacy of Becoming

I used to think legacy meant leaving something behind. Now I realize legacy is also *what you live every day*.

Legacy is the courage to show up when you'd rather hide.

Legacy is the obedience to tell your story even when your voice trembles.

Legacy is raising voices, not just books.

Legacy is helping others become who God designed them to be—by being who He designed *you* to be.

This book isn't just a memoir. It's a mirror for anyone who ever wondered if God could use what hurt them. It's a reminder that healing is a lifetime journey. That rest is not weakness. That worship can be a walk. And that when you trust God with your story, He writes beauty where there was once only brokenness.

By His Design

The name *By God's Design* isn't just a title. It's a testimony.

It's my way of saying, "God, I see You now."

I see how You used what others threw away.

I see how You turned pain into purpose.

I see how You allowed the limp so I could learn to lean.

I see how You took a little girl with walking limitations and turned her into a woman who walks in purpose.

And I know now that none of it was by accident. Not one detail of my story was overlooked or forgotten. Every piece has been part of Your divine design.

So here I am, standing on the other side of the storm—not perfect, not finished—but faithful.
Walking in purpose.
Living in truth.
Worshiping with every step.
And saying to whoever is reading this:

If you've ever doubted whether your story matters...
If you've ever felt like your pain disqualified you...
If you've ever been told to sit down, be quiet, or stay small...

Let this book be your permission slip:

You were designed by God.
You are becoming by grace.
And your story has power.

Keep walking.
Keep healing.
Keep becoming.

Not by the world's definition—but *By God's Design*.

Scripture References

The scriptures contained in the pages of this book are quoted from the **New King James Version (NKJV)** of the Holy Bible.

Scripture quotations marked "NKJV" are taken from the New King James Version®.

Copyright © 1982 by Thomas Nelson. Used by permission. All rights reserved.

Every verse was prayerfully selected to align with the heart and message of this book. May these words encourage, strengthen, and inspire you as you walk in God's divine purpose for your life.

Afterword

When I began writing *By God's Design*, I thought I was simply continuing the story I started in *Walking Limitations by Other People's Definition*. I didn't realize God was using each page to reveal how much more He had written for my life.

This book is more than a testimony—it's an altar. Each chapter marks a place where I laid down my pain, my pride, my doubt, and even my understanding, to fully embrace His plan. Every detour, every delay, and every disappointment I once resented became proof that nothing in my life was wasted.

I have learned that *walking in purpose* means saying yes to God even when the path is unclear, the pain is great, or the people around you don't understand. It means refusing to live by permission slips handed out by others and choosing instead to trust the Author of your story.

If these pages have met you in your own season of waiting, grieving, or wondering, I pray you find the courage to trust Him. You don't have to have all the answers—you only need to say yes.

I close this book with the same truth I opened it with: God doesn't call the qualified; He qualifies the called. And you, dear reader, are called.

With all my heart,
Dr. LaQuita Parks

About the Author

Dr. LaQuita Parks is an 8x International Best-Selling Author, award-winning publisher, inspirational speaker, and the Founder and CEO of **Pa-Pro-Vi Publishing**—a company dedicated to helping people take their stories from a thought to a realization. Her work is rooted in the belief that every person, living or gone, has a story that deserves to be told.

In 1976, at just four years old, a routine medical procedure changed her life forever, leaving her with a permanent walking limitation. What could have been the end of her dreams became the foundation of her purpose. Through pain, perseverance, and an unshakable faith in God, she turned her story into a testimony—and her testimony into a mission to help others heal through theirs.

Under her leadership, Pa-Pro-Vi Publishing has helped authors across the globe publish hundreds of books, including anthologies, children's literature, memoirs, and inspirational works. Dr. Parks has earned numerous honors, including an Honorary Doctorate, the Presidential Lifetime Achievement Award, the *Making Headline News* Woman of the Year Award, and recognition as an Authors Ball Award Recipient.

Her signature message—**"God doesn't call the qualified; He qualifies the called"**—is more than a quote; it is the blueprint for her life and business. Whether she's speaking on stage, coaching an author, or penning her own story, Dr. Parks leads with transparency, grace, and the conviction that healing is a lifetime journey.

She currently resides in [City, State], where she continues her ministry through publishing, speaking engagements, and her podcast, *My Heart on Pages*. Every book she writes and every author she helps is another reminder that God's design is always greater than our own.

www.ingramcontent.com/pod-product-compliance
Lightning Source LLC
Chambersburg PA
CBHW060656100426
42734CB00047B/1949